Lebron James

Interesting Facts and Quizzes About Lebron James

(The Story of One of the Greatest Basketball Players of All Time)

Rosario Balistreri

Published By **Regina Loviusher**

Rosario Balistreri

All Rights Reserved

Lebron James: Interesting Facts and Quizzes About Lebron James (The Story of One of the Greatest Basketball Players of All Time)

ISBN 978-1-77485-899-8

No part of this guidebook shall be reproduced in any form without permission in writing from the publisher except in the case of brief quotations embodied in critical articles or reviews.

Legal & Disclaimer

The information contained in this ebook is not designed to replace or take the place of any form of medicine or professional medical advice. The information in this ebook has been provided for educational & entertainment purposes only.

The information contained in this book has been compiled from sources deemed reliable, and it is accurate to the best of the Author's knowledge; however, the Author cannot guarantee its accuracy and validity and cannot be held liable for any errors or omissions. Changes are periodically made to this book. You must consult your doctor or get professional medical advice before using any of the suggested remedies, techniques, or information in this book.

Upon using the information contained in this book, you agree to hold harmless the Author from and against any damages, costs, and expenses, including any legal fees potentially resulting from the application of any of the information provided by this guide. This disclaimer applies to any damages or injury caused by the use and application, whether directly or indirectly, of any advice or information presented, whether for breach of contract, tort, negligence, personal injury, criminal intent, or under any other cause of action.

You agree to accept all risks of using the information presented inside this book. You need to consult a professional medical practitioner in order to ensure you are both able and healthy enough to participate in this program.

Table Of Contents

Chapter 1: Early Childhood 1

Chapter 2: High School Baketball 6

Chapter 3: The Pressures Of Success........ 8

Chapter 4: Eyes On The Stars, Feet On The Ground... 12

Chapter 5: Nba Career 17

Chapter 6: The King................................ 21

Chapter 7: Road To Throne 27

Chapter 8: The Decision 32

Chapter 9: From King To Tyrant 36

Chapter 10: Road To Redemption 42

Chapter 11: A Man Possessed 47

Chapter 12: Long Live King 51

Chapter 13: Early Life 53

Chapter 14: The High School Era 58

Chapter 15: Forget College. Straight To League 72

Chapter 16: "The Beginning".................. 77

Chapter 17: The Change 107

Chapter 18: I'm Coming Home 159

Chapter 1: Early Childhood

LeBron Jim: "I'm going all in to use my God-given tools and make the most of it."

LEBRON HAD NO OTHER CHILDHOOD. He was exposed and endured many hardships in his childhood. Gloria, his mother, was the only parent he had, so he did not have a father to look up too during his adolescent years. LeBron could fill this missing piece of his life with basketball. His role models would be the basketball heroes he so desperately wanted.

When she was only 16, his mother had LeBron. It was hard to imagine all the difficulties Gloria had to face while raising her child. While still a teenager with no job, no income, and no husband to take care of her child she felt completely helpless. How was she to provide a decent living for her child? It seemed impossible, and it was a huge burden. She never imagined that her child would one day become an Olympic champion and be an inspiration to millions.

LeBron Raymone James came into this world on the 30th of December 1984. His single mother moved between jobs and apartments, trying her best to keep her child safe and her own financial stability. LeBron had a very turbulent childhood. It was difficult for him to find any stability in his life in an environment that was so unstable. A child growing up in such a volatile environment would be likely to become bitter about the world. His love for Akron in Ohio, which he was born and raised there, had developed and matured over the years. Although his entire life was filled with instability and uncertainty, Cleveland was his home. Only when basketball became a part of his life did he feel able give back to the place he so deeply loved.

In order to provide some stability for LeBron, his mother made the hard, but necessary decision that he would stay with Frank Walker and move into the home a local football player. Frank had a stable, loving family and Gloria felt this was the right environment for her son. LeBron was able to feel the warmth and comfort of his family, and his love for his city and foster family only grew.

Gloria might not have realized it at the moment, but LeBron being allowed to stay with Walker was the most important event of his life. Walker was the only one who introduced him to basketball. LeBron was just nine when he was introduced by the coach to basketball. LeBron was attracted to the beautiful game from the very first moment.

LeBron was raised in a football family and became familiar with this sport. From an early age, LeBron showed that he had athletic abilities that others could only dream about. LeBron isn't just a NBA player. He's also an athlete, which is something that sets him apart from many others. Kobe Bryant and other NBA stars are best known for their basketball skills. However, their athletic abilities would be compromised if they joined any other team sport. Basketball is just their game.

LeBron didn't believe so. He excelled at any sport, no matter what it was. His incredible athleticism and tenacity would win him over any opponent, no matter what sport it was. He was an entirely new type of player. He relied on a unique skill set, which made him extremely dangerous to his rivals. We are lucky that LeBron chose professional basketball so that we can enjoy the rise of a king and his fantastic brand of basketball.

LeBron, along with his close friends, was gifted with this natural talent from an early age. They were soon in the national spotlight as young basketball players. LeBron, Sian and Dru Joyce III, along with Willie McGee, were called "The Fab Four" during their participation in the Northeast Ohio Shooting Stars Amateur Athletic Union.

LeBron's flair for drama was evident from an early age. LeBron and three of his friends decided to attend St. Vincent-St. Mary High School together. It's a Catholic private school for predominantly white Catholic students. LeBron stood out at an early stage due to his natural talents. However, LeBron and his three black friends would be even more prominent when they entered uncharted territory at their chosen highschool.

LeBron didn't mind the media attention generated by four black boys infiltrating an almost all-white Catholic school. Instead, he wanted St. Vincent St. Mary High School to become a top high school basketball player. He would be so popular that college and NBA recruits would rush to sign LeBron up for their teams. At least, that was his plan. He was not expected to achieve this, given his difficult upbringing. His childhood experiences in poverty would force him to make the best of it.

He found basketball his ticket to a better lifestyle. He knew he had the God-given tools and he wanted to create the best possible life for his family.

Chapter 2: High School Baketball

"Dream as if you'lllive forever, live as if you'lldie today." - LeBron James

LEBRON JAMES SHOWS GLIMPSES OF THE FUTURE NICKNAME. The moment he stepped onto the first competitive basketball court, he was already a star. He was first to show his brilliance in high school. As a freshman at St. Vincent St. Mary, he displayed great potential and was soon able to produce the brilliant steel that would define his celebrity status.

LeBron was a happy camper despite all the controversy surrounding his four-year-old black classmates at a Christian high school. All the attention that he had received from the controversy had become spectacle as fans and scouts all across the state began to hear about LeBron. LeBron, a small forward 6-foot-7 inches tall, has the agility of a point-guard, strength as a center, and overall basketball smarts as a coach. LeBron had all the ingredients to be the perfect basketball athlete. And many people knew that such athletes only come around once in their lives.

There were many comparisons between Magic Johnson and other NBA greats. Fans couldn't contain their excitement as they watched a legend emerge before their very eyes.

LeBron was 21 years old when he averaged 21 points, 6 rebounds and helped his team to a 27-0 record and the Division III state title. These stats improved only in his sophomore year. His points per game would rise to 25.2, while his rebounds would increase to 7.2 per minute. His fame and popularity had reached incredible heights by the end his sophomore year. LeBron would be a household name across the country, with fans coming from all parts of the state just for the LeBron show. St. Vincent St. Mary's games had to be moved to University of Akron's Arena because of the high demand for tickets. School gyms became so crowded with LeBron's fans that they were forced to choose bigger arenas. The King was already making a name for hisself; LeBron became a household name slowly but surely.

LeBron had a second stellar year of 26-1, his sophomore season. He helped his team win again the title state champions. He was honored with the title of Ohio's Miss Basketball.

Chapter 3: The Pressures Of Success

I feel under pressure. I don't put too much pressure upon myself. I feel like if my game is played well, the rest will fall into place." - LeBron James

LEBRON'S METEORIC RISE TO STARDOM wasn't without its difficulties. LeBron's junior year was difficult for him. After his two first years of high school basketball, the media attention he received began to wear on him. Additionally, the pressures that come with being "the best highschool basketball player in America right currently," according to Ryan Jones for SLAM Magazine also began to wear. His averages across all statistics was increasing with every passing year. However, this was not without its mental strain.

St. Vincent St. Mary's tragic loss in a Division II title game was the most important and poignant. It ended their back-to–back winning streak. This was devastating for LeBron as well as the school. He had been the leader in his young career and failed to win another championship. LeBron felt tired, worn out, and overwhelmed by the media storms that he was constantly facing every day.

This was The King's first major setback during his playing career. Things only got worse after that. LeBron and his team lost the Division II title. His team record was also slowly deteriorating. In his first season, LeBron had an undefeated team. Now it was a team with steadily increasing losses. Perfection is what you expect when you're the greatest high-school basketball player of all times. If you don't succeed, critics will point out, analysts will point out, and players and fans alike will begin to question LeBron's right to the throne. LeBron was failing in his duty as a King. LeBron would soon see his world crumble, even though he carried all of the world's weight on his shoulders.

Even though he was an extraordinary court player, there were still many obstacles and challenges off the court. And his junior season was starting to show it. This downward spiral made the King question his ability as a ruler. In the two years that followed, he was receiving accolade after award and attracting massive media attention. While he was still getting attention for his achievements, it was now negative. And he began to hate it. Although he would get the recognition he deserved, including being named Ohio's Miss Basketball and receiving the Gatorade National Players of The Year Award. He didn't want any part.

He was conflicted and confused and didn't know how to proceed. How many high school students were subject to the immense pressure of being a phenom at the table? He didn't know who to ask for help or guidance. LeBron even tried marijuana to deal with his continuing struggles.

High School Dropout

LeBron was even tempted to leave high school early in order to join the NBA. LeBron would be the first NBA player to abandon high school to pursue a career in professional basketball. He asked the NBA to adjust their draft eligibility rules. He thought that his large following and popularity would be enough to help him make it big. The championship game was his second failure.

LeBron became exhausted by the demands of superstardom. He was simply unable to decide what to do. He was under constant surveillance by thousands, and his recent mistakes attracted even more negative attention. LeBron saw the world as his demise and decided to make history by getting back on the basketball court.

LeBron had no choice, but to persevere with his determination and have a memorable senior year at high school. Even though he had been the target of so much negative media attention, all that was needed to make his senior year memorable was for him to show that he could turn that attention into something positive. His athleticism, natural abilities, and athleticism are still being developed. As a senior at high school, his averages would reach new heights across all boards. He was Ohio's Miss Basketball for the third consecutive season, with averages of 31.6 and 9.6 points per game.

LeBron had a new, more powerful level of play that attracted a lot of new fans. LeBron James' show became a favorite with a large crowd.

LeBron was such a popular basketball player that Time Warner Cable offered pay-perview broadcasts. He was awarded the Gatorade national player of the year award for the second time in a row. This achievement came after a career high of 52 point scoring.

Chapter 4: Eyes On The Stars, Feet On The Ground

"I believe those hard times were what made me who I am today." - LeBron Jim

GLORIA JAMES RAN UPTO HER SON AND embraced him. Gloria couldn't contain herself in her excitement despite the fact that everyone was in school.

"That's it! Take a picture of the diploma! Gloria wept, overcome, amid the cheering crowds of reporters.

LeBron, a high school graduate, just received his diploma. The same teenager who tried to drop out of highschool a year back had made a complete turnaround. His diploma was a symbol of his success.

LeBron did not let his fame on the court get to him, despite his tremendous success. His mother made it a priority to ensure that LeBron had his priorities straight. This meant that LeBron had to put school first and basketball second. LeBron was eventually influenced by this positive parental influence. As evidenced by his refusal to go on a school night with an ex-NBA player, His mother and his other support systems were there for him in times when he needed it most.

All the doubters who thought LeBron would never graduate highschool proved wrong. LeBron finished his high school career and graduated. This was the cap to one the most famous high school careers.

It was the ideal end for LeBron's highschool career and it would be the perfect opportunity to give LeBron the chance to fully grasp it after his graduation.

Stars Align

NBA Draft Lottery 2003. Russ Granik, at that time the NBA's Deputy Commissar, was responsible of drawing the lottery. Fans from all walks of life tuned in from all corners of the globe to see if they had a chance of winning the best college talent to make their teams proud. The draft was an exciting time for NBA executives and Scouts, who knew full well that it could either bring immense hope to their teams or another year of loss and disparity.

The Cleveland Cavaliers are one such team. The Cavs and their supporters were looking for a hero who could save them from their misery.

Russ Granik had three letters before him. They represented the top 3 teams in that draft. He shouted out loudly: "The Cleveland Cavaliers get the first pick in the 2003 NBA Draft."

Cavalier fans in their thousands were exhilarated. Finally, there was something to celebrate and hope for. Many Cavalier lovers turned their attention away from the television and to LeBron James, after the draft. It would be the perfect story: the young, up-and coming star from Akron playing the role the Cavalier legend's hero. After much speculation over whether LeBron should not have opted for the draft, it seemed that all the stars aligned in his favor. It seemed like he was fated to finish high school, and then get his diploma.

LeBron was one among many people who saw the draft lottery on that night. The talk of going to college suddenly stopped. LeBron had been being sought after by colleges for months. However, now it appeared that he was just a step away from something even better. He could not only be an NBA star but he was also going to be a household hero.

A New Beginning

Gloria sat down opposite the reporter as he continued to ask questions about her prodigal son. LeBron's mother was already used to it by now. Her boy's talents and work ethic were prime for him making history as one the greatest basketball players ever to play the game. Every reporter, fan, and scout wanted as much information as possible about LeBron during his climb to superstardom.

LeBron is one in a million chance to meet a player with such gifted ability. Everyone knew this, so they wanted him to jump on the basketball's biggest stage and see how he would do against the best. Every friend, reporter and fan would subtly but persistently tempt him to entertain the idea. LeBron had already fallen for it many times in junior year. After a long and difficult road, and many ups and Downs, he was now able to fully dedicate himself to the prospect that he would become a professional.

In his early years, his dreams of helping his family get out of poverty and to a better life appeared impossible. The world was focused on the high school phenom, now ready to conquer basketball's greatest mountain.

Chapter 5: Nba Career

"I treated it almost like every day was my last basketball day." - LeBron James

THE NBA. BASKETBALL'S BIGGEST STAGE. Featuring the greatest talents in basketball. It was the perfect venue for LeBron James' debut and for a future King to claim the throne. LeBron knew the time was right to announce that he was joining the league. His first opponent, the Sacramento Kings.

LeBron, his hometown team the Cleveland Cavaliers, had selected him first overall just a few months earlier. It was an exciting move that caused massive excitement not only for Cavs fans, but also basketball fans worldwide. After all the drama and controversy that LeBron had experienced in high school, it was time for him to finally make the leap to the major leagues. Some say that the NBA stands for "No Boys Allowed", and LeBron wanted people to see him not as a schoolboy, but a real threat. That was possible only if you showed up when it mattered the most. Sacramento would be your first taste of conquest.

Nine minutes into this game, the Cavs announcer unleashed the excitement of the crowd, shouting,

"Here comes the other side... This is your first James jam!"

LeBron was lightning fast and he took the ball away from his opponent. He then ran down the court and completed the feat with an impressive dunk to the delight of Cavs home fans. LeBron didn't disappoint during the remainder of the game. He put on a great show of skills, including scoring, passing and stealing.

Despite all the hype surrounding one of most talked about and media-covered league players, LeBron's performance as a rookie in the league was much better than what critics, fans and analysts expected.

His debut performance against Sacramento Kings saw him score 25 points. This is an NBA record. He had an average of 20.9 point, 5.5 rebounds, and 5.9 assist per game for his rookie year, making him one of just four NBA players with such stat lines. He also received the Rookie Award of the Year Award for his rookie year, much to the delight of all.

Fans were thrilled to have a new superstar. LeBron, who wore tattoos that included "Chosen

One", Witness and "Gifted Child", clearly enjoyed his natural prowess and showed it in his court performance. Fans were delighted to see a prodigy perform on the court. This caused waves of amazement throughout the league and in the stands.

LeBron's debut year was nothing short of amazing. His debut season was spectacular as he was one the few players to immediately go to the pros straight from high school. The rest would not be the same. Despite all his achievements on the court and his accolades, the Cavaliers were still sinking ships. LeBron had breathed new life and hope into the franchise, helping them win 18 games more than the previous season. However they were still far away from the top of the league.

LeBron would maintain this status for many more seasons. It was undisputed that LeBron was the face and voice of Cavalier, and he would bring the team the glory of winning a championship. However, as you'll see throughout his career, this feat was not as easy as his personal brilliance on court. It would be just like junior high school. LeBron would have to deal with all the pressures of the media, the doubts, and the criticisms. But most importantly, the pressures of winning a championship will allow him to shine as one among the brightest NBA talents but also transform him into one if the most hated NBA athletes to ever grace a league bench.

Chapter 6: The King

"I've always been the winner, ever since I was young. "- LeBron James

GAME 3, 2006 NBA Playoffs. The Washington Wizards was up against the Cleveland Cavaliers. LeBron had been determined and the Cavs were just a few steps away from a playoff spot. LeBron, a rising force in the league, had taken the Cavs to playoffs for the first-time in almost eight years. His leadership and prowess had finally ignited the Cavaliers' desire to win the NBA title. LeBron was now a well-known figure in the Cavs' history. He had built a reputation for himself as the man who helped them overcome hardships, trials, obstacles and got them where they wanted to be. LeBron could not wait to get back in the overtime game.

With 3.6 seconds to go, the Cavs had lost 119-120 against the Wizards. The Cavs, Wizards, and its fans knew who was going to win; it was simply a matter stopping him. The King must always fulfill the call of his people to deliver when it matters most.

"Hughes is to play it in. Found James. LeBron .... TO THE Hoop ....FOR The WIN .... HIM GOT IT !!!!

!" The Cavs announcer screamed in excitement. Cavs fans were jumping up and down, while Wizards fans panicked for no apparent reason. LeBron simply defended the game for the remaining 0.9 seconds. He didn't even have to play at that point - everyone inside that building knew that Cavs had won. LeBron was the hero of the last second.

Officially, a King was created.

LeBron had driven to baseline aggressively and hit the ball to seal the championships. It was a cold-blooded win that crushed the Wizards hopes and brought glory to the Cavs. It was LeBron's debut game winner and it was a big one. Only 2 games ago, against exactly the same team, LeBron scored a tripled in his playoff debut to stun and win over the Wizards. With his theatrical win, he would once again stun them.

LeBron stepped up to the challenge, carrying all the weight of the Cavs world. As the leader of his team, he was a force to be reckoned with and his teammates followed him. LeBron felt that he was perfectly suited to the responsibility of living up each day to this role. The King would be the definitive title that cemented this position as leader.

LeBron was no longer a sensational star. He was a genuine contender and an international superstar. He was setting records across the NBA and defining possibilities for what many believed impossible.

LeBron's performance each year would rise dramatically in just a few years. His season-long statistics would improve, with his maximum point per game at 31.4. There was much talk of LeBron becoming the MVP as he finished 2nd overall in MVP voting in his 4th NBA season. This was just behind Steve Nash. LeBron had been able to experience the joy of playing on the biggest stage for basketball in these first few years.

The King was well-versed in the terrain and now it was his turn to conquer it.

The King's Conquest

Six years had passed since LeBron James was welcomed into the league to huge admiration and support. His highlights were countless and he was a recipient of countless awards, accolades, records, medals, All-Star Game MVPs, and untiring support from his fans. His trademark chase down block became a fan-favorite. It involved him sprinting down the floor to chase an opponent, who appeared to be able lay-up or double-dunk. However, he would then throw the ball away at his opponent, completely denying him any chance of scoring. The King had just begun his rule. He had also created memorable NBA moments, which would be remembered as some of the greatest in NBA history.

One of those moments was during Game 5 at the 2007 NBA Conference Finals. The Cavs faced off against the Detroit Pistons. With more veteran players like Chauncey Blups and Rasheed Wlad, the Pistons were clearly a formidable team. The Pistons won the NBA Finals in 2004 against Shaq and Kobe, an impressive feat for a team that was no stranger to winning playoff games. According to critics and fans, they were highly favored to win. But it wasn't up for them. It was up the players. LeBron is arguably the greatest.

LeBron, who scored 48 points in Game 5 against the Pistons and 29 of Cleveland's last 30, was a historical performer, much to the delight of stunned Pistons. He was wearing the same jersey number throughout his career as LeBron, and his performance was undoubtedly "Jordanesque", symbolizing how Michael Jordan would lead his team to victory.

Chauncey Bilups, leader of the Pistons sat down in disappointment at the podium, facing a gaggle of reporters that were as stunned as he. Chauncey said, begrudgingly, "We threw all we had at his," "We couldn't keep him from moving."

LeBron was a star athlete and a pillar of the NBA. He rose quickly to the top of NBA history after only a few years. He could not let anyone stop him from achieving his lofty goals.

It was only natural that the MVP Award would be awarded to LeBron.

A crown for a monarch

Lebron led the team to a record 66-16, which was the best record in NBA history. He also averaged another incredible stat line of 28.4 points and 7.6 boards, 7.2 assists, and 1.7 steals per match. He was not able to receive the MVP award in previous seasons due to his team failing to perform to the league's standards. But this time, there was no reason to doubt that LeBron is still the greatest player in the world. He became the Cavalier's first MVP winner, with an unbeaten record and season averages.

Finally, the King had a title to his name. He would go on win three more MVPs, with relative ease, throughout his career.

This may lead you to believe that LeBron was born with a natural talent and rose to the top of the league. True to some extent, that could have been true. But superstars go through huge challenges and scrutiny along the way to greatness. The King had reached a point where he was content with all his awards. He had reached all his goals with relative ease. Now, it was time for him to seek the most valuable goal. The King wanted a diamond - a definitive crown for His Highness.

LeBron would endure the most extreme pain, agonyst, scrutiny and ultimately hatred of any athlete in sporting history. Although the road to victory was easy, it would not be easy to reach the throne or the ring.

Chapter 7: Road To Throne

"I won at each level since I began playing the game of basketball when I was nine years old. I have won at every level. But it won't be complete unless and until I win at my highest level. "- LeBron James

LIKE ALL THE LANDS LeBron has conquered with relative ease before, the quest of rings seemed extremely difficult. No one doubted LeBron's ability to reign terror on court and dominate any opponent he chose, but people began to doubt his ability to do what was really important - win. Without winning a NBA championship, no NBA legend's legacy has been fully established. All the players who won the NBA championship had something in common, including old legends such as Larry Bird, Magic Johnson, Michael Jordan and Larry Bird. LeBron had built his legacy as an heir to the throne, but to be truly part of this elite group of players, LeBron needed a championship ring.

LeBron had set his team up to be the top Eastern Conference contending team for many years. Every time they attempted to make it to the championship, they fell short. Many of these failures can be attributed the growing pains of the first couple years. But LeBron was now fully matured and fully realized in the league, and had every reason not to lose. 2010 was his final year as a Cleveland contract player. He needed to win a championship in his hometown.

2010 Eastern Conference Semifinals. LeBron had yet won the MVP award. The Cavs had again clinched a record that was the best in the NBA. This was not news to LeBron or the Cavs two years ago. However, LeBron was such a dominant player that it was now a common occurrence. Every year, the MVP awards as well as the best team record have made their way to Cleveland. LeBron, the Cavs and Larry O'Brien were aiming for a new goal.

They were due to face the Boston Celtics. The Cavs lost 3-2 after 5 games of intense back-and forth. All of their hard work this season came down to this very game. The Cavs had been arch-rivals with Celtics since their inability to advance to the Finals year after year. The Celtics had the edge, as they were more experienced with three future Hall-of-Famers, Ray Allen, Kevin Garnett and Paul Pierce. With the future fate of the Cavs at stake, the team had reached out to their King for help. However, this time the outcome would be different.

It was the 4th Quartal, with only 1 minute 20 seconds left in the game. The Cavs led by 9 points, but the Celtics maintained a clear lead of 9 points. This was the Celtics' advantage for the majority of the game. The Celtics fans gathered at TD Garden could smell blood. They were trying to get the last kill on LeBron to make him regret it and win their way to the Conference Finals. LeBron was doing his best to keep his team afloat. As a war general, LeBron took out his weapons, shouted orders to the court, and demanded the best from his team. He was desperate to keep his season alive but his personal mistakes took over.

He drove to a right baseline and tried his signature crosscourt pass towards the corner wide-open shooter.

"James... Lose it again!" Unbelievable! His 9th turnover for the night! The commentator was shocked at the spectacle of the King during the supposedly most important match of his career. LeBron was struggling under the tremendous pressure that his team placed on him, while the

Celtics calmly took down the Cavs offense piece by piece. The Cavs made one more desperate attempt at cutting into the lead by making a 3-pointer but the ball rolled in the air and out the rim almost mocking and taunting King's failure to deliver his city.

The Cavs were out of the running for an NBA title. This was not what they expected, as every player, analyst and player predicted. But LeBron had become their superstar. LeBron James' contract was coming to an end that year. Everybody knew that, if the Cavs were unable to win another NBA championship, the possibility of LeBron being fired from his home would increase. Cleveland could only keep their breath and pray for the best. Their King would choose to remain in Cleveland.

Legacy and loyalty questioned

It was a bitter ending to King's Cleveland season. He lost the ring once again. His legacy seemed to be in balance once again. LeBron had to decide if he would abandon Cleveland. LeBron smiled as he was done shaking hands with the entire Celtics roster and then walked off to the tunnels. His face was covered in disappointment. He looked down like all hope was gone for Cleveland. He faced an impossible choice. Either he would stay loyal to Cleveland, despite not winning a championship in 8 years, or he would leave Cleveland to chase his dreams in other places.

Only LeBron knew what was coming, and many Cavs fans wondered when LeBron would last wear the colors that were associated with a Cleveland Cavalier.

LeBron made that decision. No one knew what this "decision" would do to the NBA over the years.

Chapter 8: The Decision

"Maybe my pain is my motivation." - LeBron James

JULY 8, 2010: Cleveland was shaken beyond its wildest dreams. From afar, the city seemed to be in complete chaos and rioting. Flames began to fill the streets and cries of "traitor", began to echo throughout the city.

Miami was enjoying a joy unlike any other on the other end of the country. In stark contrast to Cleveland's events fireworks were lit up, posters were posted and billboards erected. You could hear the city's joy and celebrations.

LeBron's announcement, six words that were just six words, was what gave rise to this drama. The results saw the world in a frenzy not like any other. The man that had been regarded as "The King" in the past, was forced to leave Cleaveland and move to Miami. He was called "The Traitor", "The Quitter" and insulted for his decision.

Dan Gilbert was furious at the Cavaliers team owner. He addressed the fans with an open letter: "I PERSONALLY GUARANTEE CLEVELAND

VALIERS WILL WIN AN NBA Championship BEFORE SELF TITLED FORMER KING' WINS ONE."

His anger echoed those of millions of Cleveland fan who were heartbroken. LeBron hosted a live TV special, appropriately named "The Decision", just moments prior to Gilbert's violent rage. It was an announcement of which team he would play now that he is a free agent. Following his heartbreaking loss, and his disappointing season-ending defeat to what was supposed been a championship winning year for Gilbert, speculations were rampant about LeBron's future. These questions were answered July 8th.

LeBron looked calmly, but anxiously, as he sat opposite the reporter. Just a few minutes into the program, the big questions were asked.

The room was buzzing with nerves, as well as those who were watching the game from their homes that night. LeBron made a poker face as he spoke the words that would set off a massive uproar throughout the NBA's landscape. It took just six words to change the world of basketball, almost forever.

The King, the hometown hero was leaving his city. Many felt betrayed that LeBron had made such a decision. It was a sad day for the city that he had brought to its life seven years earlier. It was obvious that Cleveland was going to die. The King was moving ahead, and the hope of building an empire in his hometown was gone as he moved on to new lands to establish a kingdom.

The Big Three

LeBron was not the only one in Miami chasing his ever-elusive rings. By teaming up with Dwyane, Wade, and Chris Bosh, he formed the first modern "Big Three" of basketball. The Miami Heat had evolved from a struggling team that barely made it to the playoffs, to an overpowered powerhouse that many analysts predicted would be able to fly through the league to its Finals. This was LeBron's motivation. He wanted so badly to win that he was willing even to risk his reputation and his hometown status in order to do so. He was well aware that his legacy, as either one the most revered NBA players of all times or one of their greatest legends, would depend on whether he wins or loses in Miami. LeBron had been subject to a lot of scrutiny throughout his career.

However, with the "Decision", the scrutiny grew exponentially and there was more pressure to win. LeBron was in a delicate situation. It was unclear if he would become a true King of the game or disappoint. There was no excuse.

The Miami Heat had put targets on their backs. They had been the team to beat, with three of top players in the league joining together to dominate the NBA landscape. LeBron and Dwyane's dominance, combined with Bosh and Dwyane's quickness, made the Miami Heat the most hated team within the NBA.

With boos and jeers from crowds of fans opposing them, Miami would still win in a convincing fashion. LeBron's reputation took a 180° turn since his seven-year stint in Cleveland. He was used the attention and scrutiny that surrounded his since high school. However, he was not subject to hatred from the general public. He didn't know what to do with the millions of people who supported him. The only thing that could be done was to accept it.

Chapter 9: From King To Tyrant

LeBron Jam: "I like criticisms, they make you stronger."

LeBron was a great villain, and he enjoyed it for the entire first year of his time in MIAMI. He was known for taking victories and breaking hearts. His brazen attitude and nonchalant approach only heightened his position as the villain of this league. His status as The King had evolved to include The Tyrant, a proud and arrogant beast who was impossible to beat and whom everyone hated. Anybody who attempted to challenge him would be stopped at their feet mercilessly.

LeBron, the Heat and this attitude remained with them all the way to NBA Finals. The Heat would face an old foe in Dallas Mavericks. The Heat's team was young, athletic, confident and cocky, which is not surprising considering how they got so far in the playoffs. The Mavericks, though, were slightly older, less experienced, slower, but still had a lot on their side. Their leaders were Dirk Nowitzki (and Jason Kidd). In the 2006 Finals, Heat had met the Mavericks. It was different back then. The Mavericks had been the favorite to win the title, but Dwyane, who had lead his team over the Mavericks single-handedly, won it all. The last five years had passed and Miami and Dallas were determined to try again for victory. It was only natural that they would face each other again. This rematch was filled with the excitement and story of their previous bout.

The Heat was the favorite to win this time. They had everything Dallas had, and everyone expected Dallas to be overthrown by the Heat in the same way that they had been overpowering all other teams in the league over the past year. It was a David against Goliath game, with the Heat as the formidable giant of a player and the Mavericks as the humble but confident underdogs. In true NBA Finals fashion, Dallas would win one of the most memorable comebacks.

NBA Finals Game 2, 2011. Everything was as it should have been after a convincing win for Miami in Game 1, the NBA Finals. The Heat led by 15 points at halftime of Game 2 with their out-jumping of, out hustle and out-playing of all the Mavericks players. It was the beginning of a new Heat victory. Heat fans across the globe will always remember the sequence of events that occurred in the next six minutes.

"Terry is wide open and gets it to move," Jason Terry calmly completed a baseline jumper. The announcer was not enthusiastic about what the Mavericks were doing at that point. It seemed like everyone thought the game was finished. "Kidd flies it ahead to Terry, then...Terry the layup." With the Mavericks leading by 11 points, the Heat took a quick timeout. The Heatles seemed relatively calm despite the Mavericks' quick runs. They did not realize how quickly things would change.

The Heat had lost their lead just a few minutes before the game ended. The Heat announcer seemed suddenly more interested than ever in the game. "Nowitzki... takes it up .... PUTS IT in! 2 POINT GAME" Everyone began to sweat from worry. The Mavericks had battled back from a 15 points deficit to make it just 2 points. LeBron took over as the main focus, allowing him to once more lead his team past the hump. LeBron, the once great and ubiquitous player, was not there. Dirk just took advantage and stole all the attention.

"Nowitzki...drives...underneath lefty lay up BANKS IT IN! Dirk had just scored an amazing left-handed layup to give the lead to his team after they overcame a huge deficit in quarter 4. The Heat arena was quiet as the announcer was all that could be heard shouting excitement. Dirk Nowitzki had made a bold statement and his Mavericks were making a statement to the Heat. It was clear that they would not surrender as other playoffs teams had done. After Nowitzki's stunning victory, and Nowitzki's beautiful displays of basketball, everyone was a Dallas Mavericks supporter. Everyone thought that the Heat was impossible to beat, but once one team had done the impossible, everyone began to believe that the Mavericks would be the "heroes", destined defeat all the "villains" in the league.

LeBron Heat and his team were in a strange situation. The Heat, who had not yet lost a playoff home game, were left stunned and confused. Suddenly doubts began to creep over the players about their chances of winning the NBA title.

The Mavericks did not have to be doubtful, since once the Heat's armor was exposed, their attack was relentless. Everyone else saw the devastation that was being experienced by Heat fans, while others rejoiced at seeing the defeat they had long longed for. Everyone looked to LeBron as a guide to help them win. Just like the greats who faced adversity before him, it would be LeBron the MVP, the leader of the teams that would get them over the hump and lead their respective teams to victory. LeBron failed to live up all the hype surrounding him throughout his career. "The Chosen One," now "The Frozen One", was shrinking and freezing in the glare of basketball's greatest spotlight.

LeBron lost yet another chance to win a NBA title when the Mavericks snatched the championship from the Heat. Look at LeBron's stats from the entire series and it will surprise you that he was the same tyrannical beast everybody had feared. His 4th quarter performance was disconcerting. Instead of exerting his will on the team, LeBron scored a paltry 17.8 points per contest in the Finals. At one point, he even scored 8 points per entire game. LeBron was thrilled by the attention of the entire world. The Tyrant had now fallen off his high horses, and even though he had a stellar group to support him, the ring was not his. He had put in so much to win the NBA title and seemed to have failed.

The King that everyone once loved had become the Tyrant that everyone hated. If there was anything he could salvage from his career, it would be his honor in delivering the demands of his team - but that too had fallen into obscurity.

Lebron was willing to take on any risk in order to win. And even though he had every excuse not to, he still managed to fail spectacularly.

Chapter 10: Road To Redemption

"Don't be afraid of failing. This is how you get there.

succeed." - Lebron James

LEBRON'S FAILURE CELEBRATED AND Counted Out AT THIS POINT. He wasn't believed anymore by anyone. He was no longer the great "King", but he had fallen to the lowest point in the league. He could not win a title, and he would be regarded as an unrecognized player. LeBron's hatred, media scrutiny, and pressure was at its highest. No one believed him and he had no choice but to believe in himself. He was in his prime for someone who had seen so much success in his NBA career. He knew he still had a lot to offer, and the possibility of basketball immortality was possible.

For one season, the role as villain had been a comfortable fit for him. But it wasn't working anymore. He decided to give up his role in the NBA as the Tyrant and instead redirected all of his energy toward a single goal - winning a championship. No more games, fun, or antics on the court. He knew that if he did not succeed, his legacy would be permanently tarnished by the title "The King Without a Ring". LeBron's maturity and maturation were crucial to his redemption. He started to humble. He was no longer afraid of critics, fans, or the general public. He began to be open and others responded. LeBron understood that if LeBron didn't win a title next season, his title of "The King", would officially be lost. His legacy of disappointment will always be a bittersweet one. LeBron chose now.

The Heat dominated the league the next season, beating many teams with relative ease. LeBron's new approach to the Heat and the fact that people were getting used the Heatles was partly responsible for the calming down of the media attention and the villainous portrayal of Heat. The Heat were most concerned about the playoffs, despite surprising success in regular season. Any attempt to win the championship would be considered a failure. Everyone in the Heat locker room was aware of this fact and, since the Finals' debacle last year, were eager to try again.

LeBron had the to confront his old demons to overcome them and get over the hump. A nemesis from his past that once prevented him reaching the top of the basketball ladder was a fitting example of this. The series of events that led LeBron to his "decision", tyranny and ultimately, his downfall in the Finals were all very fitting. Lebron's tale was about to end.

Old Demons

LeBron James and Cleveland's Cavs were supposed win the NBA title in two seasons. But they were met with stiff resistance from the Boston Celtics. LeBron eventually decided to move to Miami to join the Miami Heat. Many thought that LeBron could have won that series against Celtics to win a championship. However, he stayed in Cleveland and avoided the chaos that ensued. No one was sure if LeBron could have won. But, during the 2012 Eastern Conference Finals they found out.

The Miami Heat now faced the Boston Celtics. They were the exact same Celtics who caused chaos throughout the city of Cleveland. After two seasons, many wondered if the former King was ready to challenge his old rivals. Is LeBron truly a champion player? Could he help his team when they needed him most? Did LeBron make the right choice to move to the Heat and leave Cleveland? LeBron had one last chance at facing his old demons. The only thing that was left was whether he would conquer them.

Game 6: Eastern Conference Finals 2012.

The world was counting out the Heat's return. LeBron found himself in a familiar position. LeBron lost 3-2 to the gritty Celtics after 5 games. Lebron's season could be at stake with Game 6 fast approaching. But this was not a simple 'Win or Go home' game. Lebron's career would be over if Lebron lost this game. It would be impossible to redeem LeBron for losing to the Celtics twice or coming up short on a title in two consecutive years, especially considering the incredible power LeBron has with the Heat. If he lost the game, it would not only end his season, but also his career, reputation, and honor. He was subject to a lot of scrutiny throughout his playing career. But, the Game 6 game was the most intense. LeBron had to carry the heavy burden of an overhyped Heat, which promised their fans they would win multiple championships. While he had been responsible for this load many times in his career, the burden of Game 6 was something he never had to carry.

His life was on the line. It was win or go home, but more importantly, it wasn't win, or you will be forever harmed as the laughingstock of the NBA.

LeBron must win, and face his demons. He would win them over in an inhumane, otherworldly display defiance - almost like he was possessed himself by demons.

Chapter 11: A Man Possessed

"I think about the team first. It allows me success, it allows for my team's success." - LeBron Jacob

"I'M unsure if I've ever seen LeBron as that. Not even against Detroit, when he scored 45. He looked like a man of substance that night." ESPN analyst Stephen A. Smith has a reputation for his loud and often hysterical commentary on sports, but this year he only had praise and admiration to the King. "This performance is a great one, even better than MJ's 63 against Boston."

LeBron Jam had to do it, with everything at stake. His normal playful and happy demeanour on the court had been replaced by a serious, ferocious scowl. He didn't smile, he never interacted with anyone in the arena and he was completely emotionless. He was all business right from the moment his feet touched the ground. His "do-or-die" mentality made him one of NBA's greatest players.

The TD Garden buzzed with energy and excitement as the Celtics hoped to get one more win to make it to the NBA Finals. Boston fans were familiarized with LeBron. They had been a fan favorite of insults, mockery, taunts and mockery back when he was a Cavalier. They couldn't wait for LeBron's victory again, or so they thought.

It was half-way through the first period, and things weren't going according to plan. The announcer succinctly summarized the entire situation: "Is that possible that he had a quiet 24, points? Maybe it's because it's quiet here.

LeBron's career was now in the hands of a quiet, cheerful crowd. LeBron had put on an amazing show, scoring almost half of his team's points by himself and having an answer for any punch the Celtics attempted to throw at it. One player trying to guard him was like a sheep ready to go to slaughter. It was a massacre. It was the complete demolition of Celtic pride.

LeBron's historic victory against Detroit was a reminder of his unstoppable spirit. He was determined not to let his legacy slip and ensure that his kingdom didn't lose any more. LeBron decimated his opponent this time with an emotionless, stone cold ferocity. It was a stark contrast to the Detroit game. Even though it was only halftime, LeBron's amazing performance had already drained all the energy out of TD Garden.

Chris Bosh possessed the ball and performed a post-spin move to try to score a left handed, hook shot above his defender. The ball clanked at the rim. But, out of nowhere, the announcer broke up the silence. "OH JAMES COMES FEELING IN... AND TAKES IT DOWN!"

LeBron stood out above every Celtic defender. LeBron threw a gigantic putback-dunk as a symbol of dominance to the dismaying Celtics fans. It was an appropriate play that summarized the rest of this game. It didn't matter what his teammates did that evening, regardless of whether they missed or made shots. This time, when King's number was called, the King was certain as hell that he would answer it and that no one would stop him.

Lebron was able to see past all the hype and media attention. They no longer mattered. They didn't matter anymore. The only thing that was important was the last chance to save his legacy and his career. This consumed him, eating at him every possession until it gnawed away at him. He had lost so much. He was determined to not lose the only chance he had to make right choices and his career. He had transformed and been completely removed from both his own thoughts and those of everyone around him. LeBron James had evolved from being both the arrogant villain in Miami and the cocky kid of Ohio.

He was indeed a man who had it all.

The Coronation

Lebron scored 30 point in the opening half and finished the game having a remarkable stat line, 45 points, 15 rebound and 5 assists. These statistics are only rivaled by Wilt chamberlain, who is the most successful player in NBA history. Game 6 was LeBron James' most important game. After two seasons of shrinking under pressure, he finally came up, matured, and was ready to overcome his past demons once more. The Heat defeated the Celtics in game 7 and eventually won the Finals, beating the young Oklahoma City Thunder.

LeBron's status was no longer "The King with no Ring". After nine painful, long and difficult seasons, he finally raised the Larry O'Brien Trophy to his adoring Heat fans. Everyone that had shunned his achievements had nothing left to criticize. He had accomplished all he had set out to do and the risks he took to achieve his championship had paid off. LeBron had mature, personal growth and much humility to overcome his demons and win the championship.

After winning the contest, Dorris Burke entered the podium to interview LeBron. Everyone could not disagree with the first words LeBron said: "It's about damntime."

Chapter 12: Long Live King
"I don't need too many. Glamor and all the rest

don'texcite me. I'm glad I have the game.

LEBRON'S REMAINDER WOULD CONTINUE. The Heat would reach the Finals for another season, winning yet another championship, this one against the San Antonio Spurs. Lebron's legacy was intact at this point with two Finals MVP Awards and back-to-back championships.

The Championships were an obvious coronation for The King. LeBron was now a mature, positive man with an air of calm. All those years of pain and suffering had finally made LeBron a better basketball player, but also a better person. LeBron was still fun-loving off the court and gregarious, but his seriousness toward his work ethic on and off the court made up the difference in his dominance which he continues to exhibit every day.

People know that LeBron is ready to take over the league and enjoy his role as the true King, with old stars such as Tim Duncan and Kobe Bryant about to go. LeBron has ceased all tyrannical antics. He knows that being the global basketball icon has a lot of responsibility. But, considering his life, it shouldn't be a problem.

LeBron will be remembered as one the most historic and colorful stories of our time. LeBron was a true hero on his journey. He experienced both the bitterness of defeat and the painstaking ordeals that come with it, as well the rewards of victory. LeBron can now live up to his name, having endured such intense trials during his reign.

Chapter 13: Early Life

LeBron James was birthed in Akron on 30/12/1984.

Ohio by Gloria Marie James (single mother 16 years old),

LeBron's dad (Anthony McClelland), was in and out of the house.

He spent the majority of his time in jail and was never seen again. Gloria

LeBron was raised completely by her. Growing up, it was easy to live a simple life.

LeBron struggled with his mom. Gloria bounced around

LeBron spent most of his time in retail and accounting.

Finding steady work was difficult for many. They had to

Moving from apartment to apartment is a common occurrence.

It is important to be familiar with all of Akron's major neighborhoods. This was

LeBron and the mother of his son struggled a lot.

Despite her struggles, she remained a tough person.

LeBron has a loving, supportive mother who worked tirelessly to keep him safe.

away from the violence on the streets. LeBron was

Two years ago, she began dating Eddie Jackson.

There was always trouble. Eddie was

LeBron enjoyed having a father figure to help him, but it was trouble.

Eddie was arrested for drug charges in the years that followed.

Trafficking in mortgage fraud. Gloria

LeBron was in dire need of stability.

His family allowed him to move in and be a part of the

Frank Walker, a youth-football coach, was the family member who died.

LeBron was introduced to the sport of basketball.

At nine years of age.

LeBron's serious instincts were evident from a young age

Basketball, as well as all other sports. LeBron played

He was a wide receiver in the pee wee football league.

His first year saw him score 19 touchdowns in just 6 games. Frank

Walker became LeBron's father figure. Frank

LeBron taught LeBron how to shoot. LeBron also learned.

quickly. There wasn't much that could be said for certain.

LeBron's present and future. The Walkers had three.

LeBron and LeBron have two children each, and ended up sharing their lives.

Frankie Walker Jr., a former football teammate, was in the room.

He was one of his best friend. The Walkers were a Work-class, hard-working family.

LeBron's perseverance and dedication are exemplary. They were successful.

James wakes up every day at 6:30 AM to go to school.

He completed his homework before playing basketball.

Frank slowly taught LeBron to shoot left handed.

Layups and how-to dribble. James was the one who picked everything up

Very quickly, and his skills improved with each passing day. Walker

LeBron may improve with every practice.

He quickly overtook his peers. It was easy.

LeBron was something special.

LeBron was taken in by the Walkers at Portage Path

Elementary, one of oldest elementary schools on the island

Akron. His life began slowly to shift in a more positive direction.

LeBron was much happier. With a steady

LeBron has a great family dynamic.

Focused on school and went to school every day. As the

LeBron was an AAU player for many years.

Northeast Ohio Shooting Stars. Alongside him were

His friends Sian, Dru Joyce and Willie McGee were his.

They became inseparable, and they were called

They are the "Fab Four". They promised each others

They agreed to play basketball together and attend the same high schools. The four of them decided that they would attend.

St. Vincent St. Mary High Schools.

Chapter 14: The High School Era

FRESHMAN YEAR

LeBron's swift rise to stardom began with his freshman year

year in highschool. There was a time when

Even the king was afraid, scared, and intimidated.

Before a game, play. On the night Dec.3 1999, at

Cuyahoga Fall High School, LeBron sat on the

He is anxious and nervous about bleachers

His first high school basketball match as a freshman. This

This would be his introduction for Northeast Ohio fans. James

He was intimidated, as all the players were

He was much bigger than him and he had greater self-confidence. Once the

Before the game started, each team entered the locker rooms.

Maverick Carter, a guy, spoke up for the cause.

team. Maverick was at the time the only senior starter

on the team. Maverick once again addressed the team.

LeBron felt relaxed and ready for play. LeBron

People who make him feel happy are the ones that he responds to best

comfortable. LeBron began warming up for the

game he'd already forgotten about being nervous.

The crowd was in the zone. Slowly, the crowd began to fill the gym.

LeBron was available for performance on the opening night. The

The game was fast and the Irish were in control of the early lead

At the tipoff. LeBron scored some back to back

breakaway layups, and the crowd was wild. LeBron

I was confident to perform on-the-floor with the

The older players. The first half was quick and the team was in control.

Playing together was effortless and they scored effortlessly. By the end

The Irish were up by 20 in the first half. The rest

The game was played smoothly and the Irish won.

It was won 76 to 40. James concluded the game with

For his first high, he scored 15 points with 8 rebounds.

A freshman in school varsity basketball.

The Irish won the next 26 games.

Their record is perfect at 27-0 They won the

This season was Division 3. LeBron

End of the season, average 18 points and 6.2

rebounds per game. It's a great way for you to begin your high

Basketball career in school, a perfect record, and a state title

Being the

Your freshman year, LeBron was the top scorer on your team. LeBron was

He's on his path to becoming a basketball legend in Akron.

>>>>> LeBrons freshmanyear game logs at the next page

LeBron Freshman Season Game Logs (27.0)

SOPHOMORE YEAR

Before he was even done with his sophomore year

High school and college scouts were already looking for candidates

LeBron. They immediately noticed his talents.

Athletic skills. The winning of a state title, and being named the "Best in State"

Nomination for the title of leading scorer in your team's freshman year

Easy feat. LeBron achieved an average of 25.2 points in his sophomore season.

The average game score is 22.5 points, 7.2 rebound and 5.8 assists. This is an excellent result.

His freshman year was markedly better than his previous one. It also helped.

LeBron is an elite competitor. His electrifying personality is unmatched

He began game dunks in his sophomore year.

LeBron didn't have any problem dumping on those who were protecting him

He was a tireless worker who wouldn't allow anyone to get in his way. He led the team towards a

26-1 record with another Division 3 state title

This is the second consecutive season. LeBron was simply

unstoppable. He was named Ohio's Best Young Man in that year.

"Mr. "Mr. Basketball," was the award-winning basketball team.

sophomore to do so. He was also the Ohio Governor.

"Mr. He also became the first sophomore to play basketball.

USA Today All-USA First to select player

Team. These were amazing achievements.

LeBron has been able to reach out to so many of the players that he earned their respect.

Only as a sophomore. As well as having success on

LeBron excelled in court and on the football field. He

Getting recruited for the football team.

Named First Team All-State Wide Receiver

year. Imagine that feeling. LeBron was constructing his.

Basketball resume and the building of a

Outstanding football resume. LeBron also had a stellar football resume that year.

He was simply dominant in the receiving yardage, with 700 yards.

competition.

>>>>> LeBrons' sophomore year game logs

LeBron's Sophomore Season Game Logs (26-21)

JUNIOR YEAR

After his first season of success, all

The eyes of Mr. Basketball were fixed on the next move. Everyone was focused on the next move of "Mr.

People wondered if Ireland could win another state.

title. LeBron was the talk of all things

high. Scouts from every major university attended his

To see him perform, you can play games. Home games became a popular option.

Moved to University of Akron because of high ticket

Demands from alumni, fans, college scouts, and NBA scouts.

We wanted to be there to see him play. James is in his third year.

He once again proved that he was an important contender. He

Average of 28 points, 8.9 rebound, 6 assists, 3 steals

per game. His stats were at an all time high.

It is what all basketball players dream about. He was named Mr. Basketball

Ohio. She was awarded a spot on All-USA First Team.

Also, was named 2001-2002 NBA Gatorade

Player of year. LeBron appeared also in SLAM

His national success was attributed to the magazine he published in that same year.

Exposure and everyone wanted their piece.

Despite LeBron's accomplishments in his junior year of high school,

Irish was unsuccessful in winning another state title and ended losing.

Roger Bacon High School. LeBron felt ready for the

NBA and tried for the draft declaration after the season

concluded. The problem was that he wasn't yet in high school.

He still had a year to go. He tried to petition the court for an

Modification to NBA's draft eligibility requirements, required

To have completed high school. His petition was rejected.

He was successful, and he became even more well-known.

His senior year was in full swing and he was paying attention. In the offseason

James continued to play AAU. He appeared on the cover

Sports Illustrated and ESPN Magazine. It was no

He knew his senior year was going be wild.

>>>>> LeBrons junioryear game logs at the next page

LeBron's Junior Season Game Logs (23/4)

SENIOR YEAR

LeBron averaged 30.4 Points in his senior year.

9.7 rebounds and 4.9 assists per game. His

Anyone who watched could see talent in the eyes and was skilled.

him play. Everyone asked the same question: "What?"

What would happen next LeBron had a great senior year.

There was widespread controversy and pressure that he did not comply with

expect. It started out shaky, with Gloria his mother.

LeBron's future caused problems for banks

Earning potential to be approved by them for a loan of $80,000

LeBron would like to buy a Hummer Hummer H2 for his 18th birthday.

This led to a lot more publicity, and an increase in the number of people who were interested.

Investigation by OHSAA (Ohio High School Athletic Association).

Association). People started talking and LeBron became a facilitator.

Reputation and his last high school year were now in

jeopardy. OHSAA guidelines provide that no amateur should be allowed to

Receipt any gift exceeding $100 as a reward to your athlete

performance. LeBron is introduced later in the season.

Gale and Wes Unseld accepted throwbacks jerseys

Sayers that were valued at more $900 by the

company NEXT, a urban clothing store supplier, is located in

You can exchange your pictures to be displayed in the stores.

When the OHSAA was informed about the exchange, they

This removed him from eligibility to play. This was a tremendous move.

His disappointment would cause him to lose the support of his team.

It's very difficult for the Irish in any other state to win a title

James was not available for selection. LeBron was determined.

to make a comeback.

The judge responsible for the case blocked it

The penalty was reduced from a three-game to a single game by a ruling

LeBron was allowed back to play for the remainder of

The season. LeBron's ruling made the team

One of their wins was forfeited, which led to them being

Their only loss of season.

LeBron only had one goal after the ruling.

Only focus. He wanted to return that state.

championship. Despite the turbulent Year that LeBron had

They were able to secure a state for themselves.

The title of champion. James was awarded the title following his win.

Selected to be on All-USA First Team, for a third

straight time, and was elected Mr. Basketball Ohio

Again. He also won the MVP award at The Olympics.

McDonald's All-American game. He did however lose his

NCAA eligibility since he was accepted into the program

More than two high-school-all-star events is possible

NCAA rules prohibited. James was not prohibited by NCAA rules.

He was determined to play college ball. He didn't wish to.

wait. He set his sights on bigger things. James

He stated that he would be entering the NBA draft

Avoid college basketball. Basketball would not be here without you.

The same.

>>>>> LeBrons senior years game logs are on the next page

LeBron's Senior Game Logs (25-1

Chapter 15: Forget College. Straight To League

NBA DRAFT

The 2003 NBA draft was the inaugural.

LeBron is selected by the Cleveland Cavaliers. Cleveland fans

These words will be a part of my life forever. There was much.

There is speculation as to whether LeBron will be the first.

take part in the NBA draft. LeBron was content to stay home

His hometown team and play for him. His main focus would

Be to turn around the Cleveland franchise and take them

to the NBA finals. It would be the beginning of an era.

Quicken Loans would explode for many years.

come.

The fans, critics, and endorsements came flooding in

in his first season playing for the Cavs. In his very initial game

LeBron scored 25 goals against the Sacramento Kings

Set a NBA record for scoring the most points.

First player. He was phenomenal in his first game.

game. Because he played, his fans loved watching him.

You played the game with determination, and you wanted to win. LeBron went

On average, 20.9 ppg, 5.5 rebound, and 5.9 assists

His first season was with the Cavaliers. He earned $1.95 per game. He had also a

Season high of 42 points on 3/27/04 against New

Jersey Nets showed everyone that the kid is from

Akron wanted to be here and make his mark in the game.

LeBron was a talented man, it was not a surprise. But would he be recognized?

be able re-energize the Cavaliers? The Cavs finished

The season was a disappointment with a record number of 35-47.

playoffs. Even though they missed the playoffs,

LeBron being on the roster, they played an amazing 18 games

An improvement over the previous years. It was

He made it clear that he was there for the improvement of

The team and encourage everyone to perform

better.

ROOKIE DE THE YEAR

LeBron was renamed NBA at the end of the regular-season.

Rookies of the Year. Rookie of the year: Other candidates

The 2004 Year-End Award for Best Achievement in Business was presented by:

*Carmelo Anthony (Denver Nuggets)

*Dwayne W. Wade (Miami Heat).

*Kirk Hinrich (Chicago Bulls)

*Chris Bosh of the Toronto Raptors

*Udonis Halem (Miami Heat).

*Marquis Daniels - Dallas Mavericks

*T.J. Ford, (Milwaukee Bucks)

*Leandro Barbosa (Phoenix Suns)

*Josh Howard (Dallas Mavericks)

LeBron was certainly not alone in his competition

First NBA season, many of those players competed

On a collegiate basis before entering the NBA. However,

LeBron was a very different player. He wanted the best for his family.

Establish a team spirit that places a central emphasis on the success of your organization

Cleveland should win the championship.

This would be a difficult task, and it wouldn't be simple to do.

The team would need to work together each day.

You must strive to achieve the highest level of success in order to win.

championship.

Chapter 16: "The Beginning"

2004-2005 Season

The Cleveland Cavaliers have a new and improved team

All of us are curious, what is the truth about the Akron kid?

What can be done to turn around one among the worst teams of the NBA? The

Cleveland Cavaliers opened their 20th season with the first game.

LeBron finished his second season with a 12-8 record. This was LeBron's second season with a record of 12-8.

Their previous season was a huge improvement.

LeBron had set an example and it was evident that he was following through.

The next 20 games will be crucial in turning the team around. The next 20 matches will be decisive.

Cavaliers managed their 5% retention

The record was 24-16 They were far away from being a.

The power NBA team was shocked by fans and critics

The team rebuilt and improved quickly.

LeBron's talent as a leader was evident on the court.

He was able to average 25 points and 7.4 assists per game.

rebounds per game. At 19, he was still a teenager.

That was the time. Cleveland was present at the birth

Of the King.

LeBron is now in the middle of the season.

Awarded the Eastern Conference All-Start award

Star Team. His ability to become an All Star starter.

LeBron is quickly established in his second season with the NBA

LeBron was voted as one the best players in league. LeBron

A win that saw 13 points, 6 assists and eight rebounds was a success

The West. LeBron rose to stardom as a result.

That season, Cavs wins were slower.

Although they played a respectable season, they still had to.

Improve if they had a goal to win a title.

They finished the season with a 42-40 record, but failed to win.

to the 2005 NBA playoffs. Despite the fact that he had a

The Cavs won their season and fired their head coach

Paul Silas is left with about 20 games in the regular

season for not helping team to win

streak they started the season with. They replaced

With Brendan Malone, his head coach, the plan was created.

For him to improve the record of the team so they could

Play in the playoffs. Even though the plan was not successful,

Their record of improvement is better than the previous seasons.

James's impact on the world was apparent in his 35-47 score.

Check out the team.

Season 2005-2006

LeBron had done a wonderful job improving his stats

as well as the team's record for the previous season.

He was able to improve enough that the team could win.

What about the playoffs Making the Cavs reach the playoffs.

LeBron's main focus. He wanted him to live.

You can live up to your reputation and lead your team to success.

Heading into the new Cavaliers season,

Mike Brown was eventually hired as their head coach. His focus

My focus would be to assist in shifting the Cavaliers to a top

The defensive team. The Cavaliers made the decision to add to their roster.

Larry Hughes was a dynamic point guard who averaging about 3.5 points per game

15 points per contest and was in his prime. They believed

Hughes's versatility, and LeBron's explosiveness, are both a great combination

It would work well as a team partner. With a new and improved team.

Things began to look much better under new management.

You can cheer for the Cavs.

Even though things looked good for the future,

Cavs, they started at the exact same pace as the preceding

season with a 31-21 record going into the All-Star

weekend. This was exactly where they stood.

LeBron's game stats and game played in the last season

Stealing up to the top. Moving into the All-Star

LeBron had an average weekend of 31.2 points and 6.8 assists

almost 7 rebounds per game. Those stats are impressive.

It was obvious that he would be elected All-American.

Star starter. The 2006 NBA All-Star Game saw the stars start.

Sunday, February 19th, 2007 at the Toyota Center Houston

Texas. LeBron had one of his best nights. The East was down

LeBron's explosive shooting led to 21 points in the second half.

The East won the game. The score was

With 16 seconds remaining, tie.

Dwayne Drake, who scored 20 points, won the game

The East wins a crucial layup. LeBron

He also dropped 29 points, and he grabbed 6 rebounds. His

East scored two points with their performance

Over the West It was a close match in the

The fourth quarter had more than 10 lead change events

Score ending at 122-120. It was the result of this win.

LeBron was the first All-Star MVP.

award. He would go down as the youngest ever to receive this award.

NBA All-Star MVP award to a player at the age

21. LeBron scored one of his victories.

weekend.

It was time to go back after the All-Star Weekend

Realize the potential of the Cavs and keep the focus on their improvement

Make sure they keep a record of the event so they may have a chance to participate in it.

playoffs. The Cavs were aware of how they would be treated by their opponents.

Previous seasons suffered a dip after the All-Star

weekend and determined not to repeat the mistake.

Do not make the same mistake twice. Their focus remained off, and the Cavs

In fact, they lost five straight games following the All-Star

weekend. LeBron finally had the opportunity to showcase his talent.

Your talents can help you pull your team out of the mud and get them back

for success. LeBron's leadership will ensure that you succeed.

Cavs had a 9-game winning streak.

They are now back in the playoff race.

The Cavs had finished the season.

seven-year steak. They had made it to the playoffs.

They finished the season with a 52-30 record.

LeBron received All-NBA First Team Honors.

His first career record. He was also one the youngest

It has been awarded to players from all walks of life.

James had achieved something that seemed impossible.

It is impossible to reach critics, fans, or even some of the Cavs owners. He had purchased a failing NBA franchise.

They were able to get them to the playoffs in just 3 years

He wanted to be a part of the league. He was creating a new basketball league.

You will have a resume that rivals Kobe Bryant's.

Michael Jordan. He wasn't just a basketball legend.

Was a local hero and legend.

In the first round, the Cavs were victorious.

Washington Wizards. In the regular saison

The Wizards had defeated 3-1 the Cavs. They were a great team.

Cavs would be the most dominant offensive team.

They should be prepared to step up their defense, if they have any plans.

They won the playoffs. The Wizards had

A solid roster. They had one their deadliest shooters

Gilbert Arenas, a member of the league, was selected. He was in

He was at the peak of his career and was a formidable opponent.

Antawn Jamison (6'8") was their power forward.

Who averaged 20 points per match and who had not

This season, I missed one game. Another prominent

Caron was the Wizards' only player at the time.

Butler, a 6'7 small forward, was averaging 17 point per game

It was a good game, and he was a solid defensive play. In round one

LeBron was unstoppable throughout the playoffs. He

You scored 32 points, 11 boards and 11 assists. A triple

It's a great way to kick off your first playoff.

appearance. It was a testament of his dedication

For making the Cavs a winning team. The rest

They were not easy opponents to the Wizards in many of their games, but

LeBron was a leader that drove the team to victory. He

This averaged 35 points and 5.7 assists with 7.5 rebounding

His first round of playoffs. He was a success in the eyes of critics and fans alike.

He could perform when pressure was on. The

Cavs won and were now ready to face

They will be taking on the Detroit Pistons as their next opponent. The Detroit

Pistons were Eastern Conference champions

The Cavs knew from previous seasons how serious of an injury it was.

They would be their opponent. They had the best record in

The Eastern Conference had 64 wins that season and 18 in the following season.

losses. The stakes were very high and the pressure was intense

Perform was even more.

The Pistons were keen to have another go at it.

The title was the same as it had been in the previous finals

season to San Antonio Spurs. Both would go.

They were down without a fight. Pistons had an experienced team of

Ben Wallace, Rip and Hamilton were the main players

Rasheed Wallace (Tayshaun Princess) and Chauncey Bluffs (Chauncey Billups).

They were not strangers to the playoffs.

championships. They won the NBA title in 2004, and they were crowned NBA Champions.

They wanted more. The first two games were won

Pistons quickly followed and people began asking if

This would lead to a sweep of the next four games. Next

Two games the Pistons became a little too comfortable during

The Cavs' defensive end and the Cavs leveled the series.

2-2. The Cavs won their next game and took the title

Doubts about their ability to perform in opposition to the

Pistons quickly vanished. The next game proved to be extremely exciting.

Close, but Pistons won 84-82. The series

The score was now 3-3.

Auburn Hills, Michigan, for Game 7.

James started Game 7 with a great start.

He went on to score 10 goals from his 15-field goal attempts.

The first game's second half. He lost the first half of the game.

His first seven shots of second-half scoring were missed.

Just 1 of 9 occurred in the third quarter and fourth quarter.

This gave them a substantial lead over Cavs.

They won the game, 79 to61. LeBron

Averaged 26 points, 8.6 rebound and 6 assists in 7

game series. The defense by Pistons was simply too much

in Game 7. Despite their loss, they had

James's performance was outstanding throughout the season

His game at all levels. The previous was almost defeated

Eastern Conference Champions, it was obvious that

Cavs and James were constantly changing. James was active in the off season.

He was determined and focused to improve his craft.

Take on the title. LeBron and Cavs were in the future

Looking bright.

Season 2006-2007

LeBron showed his fans this season that he is indeed a good actor.

He was one of the best players the league. The Cavs were eliminated

They finished the regular season with a 50 to 32 record, just like they did in their previous season

The previous year. They now wanted to focus on

reaching the NBA finals. LeBron averaged 27.3 Points

6 assists and 6.7 rebounds per contest Each

LeBron showed significant improvements in his season

team to new heights.

The Cavs were back and they were in the playoffs

They were determined for the finals. They started the playoffs

Much like the year before. They had to deal with the

Washington Wizards in the first round that sparked

A competitive rivalry was formed at the beginning. Going into

This year's playoffs, the Cavs played as one cohesive unit.

The Wizards were swept in just 4 games. The team

Was focused, hungry and ready for a chance at the title.

The Cavs won the second round in the playoffs.

Faced the New Jersey Nets. The Nets won.

It was a solid team, with many veteran players who were not

There were no strangers to the playoffs. All-Stars were featured in the Nets' playoffs.

Jason Kidd, Richard Jefferson, and the other half-backs

Vince Carter: Half-man, half-amazing Vince Carter It was evident that

This round would be full high caliber playoffs

Competitions and highlights would be shown

ESPN will be around for many more years. The series began with a very tight start

Each game was close, and the scores stayed that way. Even

Although the games were close, however, the Cavs defeated the Nets

In six games. LeBron, the Cavs and their team were heading to the

Eastern Conference Finals to Face an Opponent

They were well-versed in the Detroit Pistons. Going into

Finals: The Pistons were deemed a better team

They were better than the Cavs. Even though the matchup round had been

It is different. The series started the same as last year.

Detroit took full advantage in the first two home games

And won them both. The first game was a great success.

James had a disappointing start and was eliminated from the playoffs.

Only 10 points It was obvious that the Detroit

The Pistons were strong as a defensive team. The Cavs were

They weren't aware they were the same.

predicament was the same as in the previous year and we knew that

They needed to work harder if they wanted to get a shot at it.

The title. The criticism came from all angles.

LeBron and Cavs James would recover however.

Games 3 & 4 were decisive for the Cavs' win. Game 3

James had 32 points and 9 rebounds as well as 9 assists to take the lead

The Cavs beat the Pistons by 88 to82. Next

LeBron game dropped 25 points and 11 assists to win with 7 boards

Cavs to win the series 91-87 The series was tied

At 2-2, LeBron was back. LeBron was able to prove his fans in Game 5.

It was criticised that he was King. The game was very.

Each quarter was close to its end and more than 10 lead were present

The second half saw some major changes. The Cavs concluded

In an intense double-header, the winning score was 109-107

overtime battle at Palace of Auburn Hills LeBron's

This was a performance that was simply legendary. Halfway

LeBron had 21 points into the 4th Quarter, while the Cavs had 23.

They went up 79-78. LeBron began a scoring streak.

All who watched were baffled. In a post-game

Interview with the Pistons point guard following their loss

Chauncey Blups was interviewed about LeBron.

performance. He responded by saying the following.

"We just threw everything we had at him.

But he couldn't stop himself." In less 16 minutes

LeBron continued scoring 29 of the Cavs' thirty points.

The team's 25th and final points from 11-of-13 shooting

The field. The game was forced into overtime by an

With only 9 seconds remaining, this electrifying dunk is the best of all game. The game ended up in a second overtime.

LeBron was the driving force behind the team's win.

Score a layup and get in the lane with just 2 seconds

remaining. It was a playoff performance.

As legendary, it was written down in the books. LeBron ended the

Night with 48 point, 9 rebounds and 7 assists Cavs

Pistons led now 3-2 and were just one game away

From becoming the Eastern Conference Finals champs.

James made NBA history, becoming one of the greatest players in the NBA.

Most talked-about athletes in the entire world. The Cavs were eliminated

In game 6, the Pistons lost to them with a final score in excess of

98-82. LeBron finished with 20 points.

8 assists and 5 rebounds. The Cavs had accomplished it. They were

The San Antonio Spurs will face us in the NBA finals.

The San Antonio Spurs were a skilled and experienced team.

The disciplined team was known for its ability to win the NBA

championships. Going into the finals, the Spurs were

They were highly favored to win. They were more

They had the experience and knowledge to help you succeed.

win. Their goal was to end LeBron

defensively. This was definitely a simpler task than expected.

done. They were aware if they could contain LeBron's scoring

They would be able dictate the game's pace. They could also dictate the flow of play.

Spurs were able to begin the finals strongly by winning

The first match was 85-76. LeBron was held scoreless by them.

This forced him into taking tough shots in the field.

Could not get on. LeBron suffered terrible shooting

night, making 4 of 16 shots that he attempted. The Spurs

Experience and discipline were the keys to success.

The Spurs continued their winning streak with the two remaining games.

With a 3-0 advantage over the Cavs, they dominated and prevailed.

James got to see the finals of the NBA elite Finals.

As it appeared. LeBron still showed glimpses

brilliance. The Spurs were prepared and knew what to do

Respond to everything that he offered. The strong

Tony Parker and Tim Duncan have the experience and leadership to lead.

Bruce Bowen, Manu Ginobili, and Bruce Bowen could also be a good choice.

LeBron was a great player for the Cavs. The Spurs came out victorious.

After a 4-game sweep of the Cavs, the Cavs were defeated by the defending champions and the team was named the

2007 NBA Champions. LeBron continued his training in the

Inoff-season and available to take another shot at the

championship in the following season. Even though

Cavs lost. It proved they were a high caliber group

Who was capable to win a championship.

2007-2008 Season

The Cavs knew it was possible to use some

Their lineup has been improved to provide them with a better experience

It is essential to have a winning edge. They needed a strong defensive

Adjustment in their lineup if they plan to beat another team

As the Spurs in their finals. It was no surprise that they stuck.

With their current selection of LeBrons, Ilgauskass, Gooden

Pavlovic, Hughes

Strong teams were established in the 2007-2008 seasons.

form in Western Conference and the Cavs necessary to

To remain competitive, they had to adapt. It was the

Kevin was the Boston Celtics' first ever teammate in 2004

Garnett, Paul Pierce and Ray Allen. They would get

"Big 3" is the name of the team. It was obvious that the Cavs did not belong in this "Big 3".

It helped to improve this season and prompted a midseason

To help them improve their performance, they can trade. They

Drew Gooden and Larry Hughes ended up being traded.

Delonte and Ben Wallace. They also went on the to

Wally Szczerbiak is a former shooting guard.

A great addition to Cavs.

The Cavs now have a new roster.

The regular was not easy to adapt to and the staff ended it.

The season ended with a record of 45-37. They had won 5 of their games

Less than the previous seasons and the critics started to give their verdict.

talk. LeBron averaged 30 points during a very successful season.

7.9 rebounds and 72.2 assists per game. This is what it would look like

enough to see the Cavs reach the finals? The big 3,

Boston had an outstanding season with a record 66-16. It was unforgettable

The league's record for the season was outstanding and it led to

Everyone is aware that the Celtics had their sights set upon the Celtics.

The winning of an NBA title

The Cavs opened their first round of playoffs on just

As the previous two. They faced the Washington Wizards.

This year's rivalry was quite different. Some players took on

LeBron was considered an overrated Wizard by the Wizards.

player. LeBron is no stranger to the skeptics.

You answered strongly with 32 points to lead this game

Cavs to a win at Game 1. The series was decided in Game 6.

The Cavs were the superior team with 105-

88 victory over Wizards The Celtics were a tremendous team.

This was a dominant team that was in the middle if an intense

Seven-game series against the Atlanta Hawks. The Cavs

It was known that if the Celtics lose to the Hawks, they would

You would have a tremendous advantage to win in the Eastern

Conference Finals once again. The Celtics came out on top

Game 7: The Hawks It was evident that it was

it will be nothing short of a fight to advance to

finals. The Cavs played average in the regular season.

Season, they were playing very well during their first round

playoffs. Could they play well enough to win?

The Celtics are out!

The TD Garden hosted both the first and second games.

Boston and the Celtics did their best to make use of this opportunity.

Chapter 17: The Change

Everyone understood that James wanted the best.

You will leave a legacy in basketball that will be cherished forever

For many years to come. The real question was whether he would be.

You were able build that legacy with Cavaliers? Which team

James could be given the best opportunity

What can you do to maximize his talent? Are the Cavs going to be a

Continue to chase something or join a championship team

They couldn't reach them?

There were many unknowns and questions.

LeBron and Cavaliers fly from all angles. LeBron

Had to make a choice that would be best for all parties.

Not only for him, but also his family. It was a free agency.

LeBron had an abundance of options and teams.

All the parties were open to offering him a substantial contract. All

New Jersey's top-tier NBA team, the New York Knicks.

Nets and Miami Heat, Chicago Bulls, LA Clippers and Chicago Bulls were all ready

LeBron is open to you. Each team could offer something.

LeBron made millions of dollars and they had their own star

The franchise would not be necessary to create players for these types of players

LeBron's talents are the only focus. Take, for instance, the New

York Knicks have signed Amare, a ferocious player from the United States.

Stoudemire, at the peak of NBA basketball career.

This combination would be unstoppable. The Chicago Bulls

Had a young team including Derrick Rose and Luol Ding.

Joakim Noah. The advantages of a young team are many.

each have their own set of challenges, but also the potential to last.

It is a term that refers to a successful match. It

LeBron would also play on this same stage.

Michael Jordan, the great basketball player, continued his efforts. Critics

LeBron fans often compared him to MJ.

It was an exciting opportunity to play for Bulls. Los Angeles Clippers

It is also very intriguing because they were a

Problematic franchise. LeBron being their representative

Fans hoped for rescue. But it would not.

LeBron would really like to go through all the pains and struggles

You are trying to rebuild a franchise that is failing? It was clear that

LeBron had one central focus: a team that wanted to succeed.

To win a title. It was something completely different

LeBron sensed that the Miami Heat was a threat and started to recognize it.

They may be the best possible fit.

The Miami Heat did not have the best record in the NBA.

The same historic achievements as those of the older generation

Franchises like Chicago's Knicks and New York Knicks

Bulls. They did share a vision however that was in line

LeBron's. They wanted to make a championship.

team. The Miami Heat team was competent and experienced

Staff who were ready to do whatever it took to make the job easier

Create an unstoppable business empire. In past history,

Pat Riley, the Miami Heat's head coaching coach, had previously been with the club.

Strong history of building champion teams. He was

Widely regarded as one the greatest coaches of all-time.

Dwyane Watney, the Heat's all star point guard, was also part of the team.

He had extensive experience in both the playoffs und in the finals.

finals and had also been awarded a Miami Champion title

2006 Chris Bosh was free to act in 2010 during the free agency

You joined the Miami Heat team. The Miami Heat were

They are expanding their franchise to be a stronghold and if

LeBron joined because he believed he would be the most important member of the team

they could be considered for a championship.

LeBron wanted to be retained by the Cavaliers, so they made

He received a huge salary offer of 30 millions per year. They also

Chris Bosh was a free agent and we tried to get him onto the team.

agency to enhance the Cavaliers' potential, but that

It didn't turn out to be a good idea. The Cavs want to keep

LeBron and his family were looking tired in their hometown. The question is:

King actually left his hometown with everything that he owned.

built? Many sources claim that James actually

Would he be willing to leave Cleveland?

It's worth another year to chase a championship

This was not within his reach.

LeBron received something in Miami Heat

They couldn't do it for other organizations. They offered him

Your best chance to win a championship. Pat is your coach

Riley has won several championships over the years.

Dwyane, Miami Heat pointguard Dwyane

Recently won a championship at the Miami

LeBron seemed to prefer Heat. They had the

LeBron was missing the pieces he wanted. The winning

Pat Riley, experienced.

Dwyane Watkins, champion point guard

LeBron did his thing on ESPN's July 8th 2010

official decision and an announcement to all the world. "

This fall, I plan to bring my talents down to South Beach

You can join the Miami Heat. LeBron's passing was shortly followed by the Miami Heat.

announced and decided, critics and fans

The result was absolutely wild. They began to slam LeBron.

Being uncommitted, weak, or even calling him an An.

An average player. The backlash he received

This was one of the most resentful sports fans in history.

People began throwing rocks at his jersey after he was burned by them.

billboards, posters, and more. People from home slowly become more familiar with their surroundings.

He was initially portrayed as an evil villain. He was one.

Most beloved athletes in all of the world, but with he decision to

His departure from the Cavs made him one of the most hated.

These are the most important players from all time. Dan, Cavs owner

Gilbert wrote LeBron a letter of love.

Many names were given to him. He was able to say

It was impossible for the Cavaliers to win a championship.

LeBron joined the team.

Despite the severe backlash LeBron experienced,

It was the right choice for him at that moment. He was now

On a team that is built to succeed over the years.

LeBron was optimistic about his future with the Miami Heat.

Season 2010-2011

LeBron was in his first season of the 2010-2011 Season.

The league's most talked-about player. He was

The season is heavily scrutinized and many factors are taken into consideration.

Many people hoped he wouldn't win a championship.

Heat. LeBron wasn't the only star player

That forced him to leave his team. Carmelo Anthony resigned from the Denver

Dwight Howard and Nuggets have left the Orlando Magic.

What was the reason LeBron received such a backlash

While critics and fans were treated equally, other players were treated fairly

For your departure? LeBron was the city's choice for their

Their sports icon, their hero and savior in the hometown When

Fans felt as though he had abandoned the city after he left

It was where he comes from. It was a more personal touch.

James. James was asked in an interview what he thinks about James.

Consider the Miami Heat. What would they do?

accomplish. James said that he believed in the power of teamwork.

They believed that they would win multiple rings. This led to further

This fan-fire was evident in the majority of the

away games that were played by the Heat during that season. Fans would

Boo James at the free throw line.

When he entered, things were clear to him. LeBron

He knew that he would be the subject of criticism.

However, it was not as severe as he had anticipated.

To add more pressure to the blaze, the

Heat started their season poorly. Nearly twenty

Heat team started their first season together with games

With a 9-8 Record. It quickly became one of our most beloved records.

We talked about things in NBA. LeBron was gradually

He adjusted to the style and play of his team. They

Slowly, we began to work in concert with one another.

Halfway through, the teams started blowing each other away

season. Chris Bosh. Dwyane Wallace and LeBron Jim

Start to click on the court and become

unstoppable. LeBron began to realize that he could count on it.

It was better to be supportive of his teammates than it was to be in total.

He took charge of the game. He was able to take charge of the game when it got hard.

Dwyane's speed, agility and speed will help you get there

You can do serious damage by putting your basket in the basket. Bosh could help him to play

It is both a dynamic center and a power forward.

Depending on whom they faced. They all faced the same person.

They were so adaptable that they won games with them

Slowly, the critics were forgotten by ease. The critics

We wanted to see Heat fall. But they did.

opposite. LeBron joined the Miami Heat for his first season.

Averaged 26.7 point, 7.5 rebound and 7 assists per

game. He was closer and closer to averaging.

triple double. Heat takes place in the middle of the season.

A team meeting was held. They discussed the importance

Their first season as a couple and what they needed

You should work harder to win more games. They began

to turn things around. They won 21 of their

Next 22 games. It was a testament of their dedication.

Make the Eastern Conference the best team

season. As the season progressed, Miami

LeBron's leadership saw heat improve. In

LeBron had a month of February 2011

He had his best career performance. He dropped 51

The game was won by 11 rebounds and 8 assists. It was amazing

performance.

James,

Bosh, Wade and the rest of the 2011 team were selected

All-Star team. It was a tremendous accomplishment to have three of these players.

All-Stars are from the same group. The East came out victorious.

Losing the All-Star match 143-148 to West that year

Kobe was named All-Star Player MVP. The Heat

You continued to play hard for the rest of your season.

playoffs and ended the season with a total of 58-24

record. Despite being shaky at first, it has steadily improved over the years.

Season, the Heat reversed course and were ranked

The Eastern Conference's 2nd-ranked team

Chicago Bulls One of the best Bulls seasons ever!

The record for the seasons since MJ is 62-20. This season was the

The league MVP award was awarded to Bulls point young Bulls.

guard Derrick Rose.

It was now that the Miami Heat had to step up.

Perform in the playoffs. Going into the 2011 playoffs

LeBron James and his critics received a lot hateful criticism from the

Heat. It was clear that the fans wanted to see it.

The playoffs bring down the Miami Heat.

In the opening round, the Heat faced the Philadelphia76'ers.

They quickly proved they are serious about business and were quickly beaten.

The Sixers won 5 games.

Their next matchup demonstrated how amazing they were

were. LeBron and his team were their next opponent.

was very familiarized with, the Boston Celtics. The Celtics

They had a history with James in the previous playoffs

bouts. LeBron knew their game well and was

They are determined not to allow things to repeat. The Heat

You can watch some of the most thrilling basketball games that fans have ever seen.

had seen. Miami was not up to the challenge of the Celtics big 3.

Even though the Celtics lacked the experience and tenacity,

LeBron Jam and the Heat are necessary to win.

They were defeated. The Heat won the series.

In 5 games. This was the first of five games.

LeBron's first ring is won in his second year. Next Chicago Bulls.

It was a great achievement by league MVP

Derrick Rose and his team will make it to the Eastern Conference

finals. He was an absolute star of the playoffs. Rose was

The Heat considered him a serious threat because he was an extremely dangerous player.

explosive point guard. He could also shoot from outside.

The Bulls were able to penetrate the rim with incredible speed. The Bulls were

The defense was outstanding and the result was obvious.

It would be fun to follow series. The Heat lost.

Game 1 against Bulls 103 to 82. It was a complete.

blowout which left fans and analysts puzzled.

How could the Heat be so poor? LeBron was an actor.

A terrible game with 15 points (6 rebounds, 6 assists).

The Heat simply couldn't take the Bulls' defense.

Game 1. Game 1.

Heat needed to shift their attention back to the original

Just win the games with a game plan

There were serious concerns.

The Heat's inability to defeat the Bulls. Game 2

It was a bad start for the Heat as the Bulls won

Heat 26-19 at halftime. LeBron

Was determined to win and it was evident in the second-half

the game. LeBron led Heat with 29 points.

The driving force of the win was 5 assists and 4 rebounds.

fourth quarter to help Heat get the win. The Heat

The fourth quarter was won by the Bulls with only 10 points

Quarter: LeBron scored 9 from his 29 points in this quarter

Final 5 minutes, fourth quarter. LeBron was

Key factor in helping the Heat win Game 2 was his leadership.

He turned his attention to Derrick, the lightning fast defense.

Rose. Rose.

Score: 96-85. LeBron concentrated on driving to

Chicago must win Game 3 by scoring one more point to be in early foul

trouble. Bosh could also get it.

As he drove up to the lane, he created more

Scoring opportunities for the team. Bosh had a successful career.

In Game 3, 34 points were a record post-season high.

LeBron also was able to close down Derrick Rose

The fourth quarter is defensive. Force him to take off-balance shots.

Game 4 was another high stakes game.

LeBron managed to get things back in his hands. Dwyane Wade

LeBron & Bosh helped me through the majority of the game.

through. LeBron finished with 35 points and 6 rebounds. He also had 6 assists.

Bosh scored 22 points, 10 rebounds, and 1 assist.

Game 4 ended up in overtime and James had the final word.

deliver. LeBron shut down Derrick Rose during overtime

The Heat won the game by winning defensively

101- 93. The Heat were one game away

Being Eastern Conference Champion and

We are now heading to the finals.

LeBron scored 28 more points in Game 5.

The Heat defeated the Bulls with 11 rebounds.

83-80. The Heat became Eastern Conference Champions

And were going into the finals. The Heat stood to face

The Dallas Mavericks won the finals. They were a premier

One team that was always able to make it to the finals.

Could this be LeBron winning his first award?

championship? The Dallas Mavericks were an

Team members who were experienced and prepared to do anything

That championship will be won.

LeBron had 24 assists in Game 1 (2011 NBA finals).

Scored 9 rebounds and 5 assists. LeBron did well in his game

Night behind the arch, hitting 4 of his 5 shots

Pointers for the evening The Heat went on winning

Game 1 had a final score between 92 and 84. LeBron

That was the beginning of the taste of victory. Game 2 was played.

Different game for the Heat. Dwyane was Wade

A great Game 2 with 36 point, 5 rebounds and 6,

assists. The Heat did a great job in the fourth quarter

With an 88-73 win over the Mavericks and a little more,

There were 8 minutes left. Heat felt like the had it all.

The bag is empty. What happened over the next 8minutes?

Fans baffled and everyone else watching the game. The Dallas

Mavericks scored in an erratic fashion in the last eight minutes.

The Heat didn't respond quickly. The Heat began to crack

Dallas Mavericks played defensively in the fourth quarter.

It was ultimately won 95-93. People couldn't believe their eyes.

Heat game 2 was lost by the Heat They needed to be serious

concentrate. This was the NBA finals. You can't let your guard

You can't even slip up for one minute.

The Heat had to regain control of their focus.

Perform in Game 3. LeBron was an average performer in Game 3.

Performance with 17 points. 3 rebounds and 9 assist.

This is a 6 out 14 shot. Dwyane had a

Clever performance with 29 points. 11 rebound and 3

assists. Was the pressure of the finals too much?

LeBron to take care of at this moment? Chris Bosh & Dwyane

Wade took LeBron's place.

Chris Bosh hitting was a key factor in the team's win

The winning shot. The Heat won Game 3.

Final score of 88 to 86

Game 4 was another closely contested game.

LeBron's worst performance. The

Mavericks held LeBron at 8 points, 9 rebound and 7 points.

assists. LeBron's situation could not have been worse

Game 4. They just put him down defensively.

LeBron was unable get any shots of Fall. The Heat continued

To lose Game 4 with an ending score of 8683. If LeBron

The Heat could have had the most satisfying performance if it were even half as good.

Likely won Game 4. LeBron had half of the turnovers that he

Points. He needed to significantly improve his performance.

They would lose that title. The series was now tied at 2-2

It was still unclear who would win 2011

NBA championship. The pressure to perform was high.

James must bounce back in Game 5 to prove he is serious

About winning a title.

James did a great job in Game 5 and was able to keep his cool with a

Triple double: 17 points, 10 boards and 10 assists

assists. LeBron started the first period aggressively.

But he ended the game completely passively. He did

Not attack the paint in the second half.

Limiting himself to poor jumping shots. Dallas's zone defense was

Too much for James & the Heat. The team didn't adjust.

It did so and was ultimately defeated in Game 5. The final score was 112-103.

The Heat were in trouble.

The Heat were down by 3-2. It was now time to celebrate.

LeBron to perform in front of the world, proving why he's "The."

Chosen One". LeBron began Game 6 with a hot start. He won.

He took his four first shots and scored nine to win the contest.

Heat an early 20-11 lead LeBron was a young man when he started.

He would score only 12 points during the rest of the game.

The game. It started to look like he was giving it up.

Like Game 3. He was taking bad shots and was not being able to catch the ball.

To get the job done, he drove down the lane until he was satisfied

to be productive. The Mavericks performed better than

Heat. They were able to distribute the ball efficiently and made

These were crucial defensive stops when they really mattered. LeBron ended

The game was won with 21 points. There were 4 rebounds and 6 assists. The

Heat lost Game 6 by a scoreline of 105

95. The NBA's 2011 Champions League was won by the Dallas Mavericks.

Champions.

It was an awful way to lose in the finals.

LeBron was aware that they did.

In the offseason, there is much to do. As always, the

The sports world was abuzz with hypothetical what-ifs

Analysts, commentators and critics follow the Heat's progress

Mavericks' loss. It was evident that the

Mavericks was a hard team to beat. There were so many.

Many ways that Heat failed to perform left many to be surprised.

They should be asking themselves if winning is something they really care about.

championship and LeBron's ability to respond to the

Tension of the finals. LeBron able to finally succeed?

Next season win a championship or would he

He was stuck trying to reach a dream that was beyond his reach.

Season 2011-2012

There was no question that Miami Heat were the best team in the world.

Talented Team. They had made it all to the NBA

Finals are a great achievement. The

The Finals were the catalyst for the Big 3 to begin to unravel.

Many questions have been raised about their chemistry. LeBron and his wife

embarrassing performance in Game 4 People began to

Question whether he can handle the pressure

It's all part of the finals. This wasn't the second time.

LeBron started to lose his strength during the finals bout.

Many critics wondered when the King would win.

championship. The Miami Heat still had a great season.

regular season from the previous years and made it to the finals.

It didn't matter. People were so focused only on the facts

LeBron missed his chance at winning a title

These other accomplishments were the beginning of his career.

overlooked. LeBron became a household name in the weeks after the finals.

Totalement isolating himself from anyone to reflect on

What had gone wrong. LeBron was forced to think deeply about what had gone wrong.

It's not just about his performance. It's the entire dynamic.

The team. LeBron was aware that he wouldn't win.

All the glory to himself. If he could improve,

The Heat team's chemistry would have been a lot better.

Greater chance of winning this title. Feeling the weight

Dwyane Wade lost his job and reached out LeBron to help them.

We could all sit down together and develop a strategy.

You should push them to win a championship. Dwyane Drake suggested that

LeBron should be the primary leader of the group. Bosh James and

Wade was already the key player in the team's success, but

They didn't have a primary leader before.

season. Dwyane thought that this was their primary

downfall. LeBron was needed by the Heat to be who he was.

Cavaliers. LeBron was needed to lead them.

for the team, the visionary and the person who

It would encourage the team to work towards greatness. After

He let go of the past, and he began to see things from a different perspective.

LeBron was ready for a new reality. He wasn't

He was ready to play for the win in basketball.

Ready to be great.

Heat got a new outlook and focus.

They are determined to win a championship in this year. They made

They made some minor changes to their lineup that resulted in an improvement

Their team dynamic. They added a veteran player

Shane Battier is available to assist with improving their starting five lineup.

Battier had the experience.

A leadership mentality that emphasizes teamwork

improvement. Rockets was his great leader

Heat and the Grizzlies, and would help them keep their

Maintain your composure when faced with high-pressure situations.

The Heats 2011-2012 Season would be on

There was an NBA lockout.

year. The NBA lockout 2011 was the 4th such lockout.

NBA history. The lockout was 161 days long, beginning at

July 1 to December 8. The main issues with the lockout

Was the division revenue and how did the salary cap

Structured the luxury tax. The proposal was submitted by

Owners desired to decrease player-related revenue

Income as low as 57%, but up to 47% Counter Offer

53% was the average percentage for players. The owners fought back.

Would like to have a luxury tax and a salary cap.

In an effort to increase the competition between them, players

franchises. Both sides ultimately failed.

An agreement was reached that led to the NBA cancellation

All preseason games through December On November

26. They eventually reached an agreement which would

End the lockout They reached an agreement to end the lockout.

A revenue split of 49%-51.2% with a flexible salary cap but

A stricter luxury tax enforcement.

LeBron and others were still available to help despite the lockout.

The Heat went hard and kept improving on every occasion

angle of their game. The lockout began on the day it was implemented.

LeBron proved why the King was he. He raised 37

For the team, points, 10 rebound and 6 assists.

In the finals, they were beaten by the Mavericks. Despite being defeated in the finals by them, the Mavericks prevailed.

A shorter season meant that the team was playing better

This was a marked improvement on the previous season. They were consistent with their pace

and was able control the flow in each game. At the

LeBron ended the regular season at 27.1 points

He averaged 7.9 points and 6.2 assists each game. His game performance improved.

Leader and the team concluded the season with a 46-20

record. LeBron also won his third MVP

It was the season's highest honor. LeBron saw the best of both worlds.

The Heat was out, it was time for playoffs to begin.

again. They knew that they could reach the finals.

They didn't give up. They had no choice but to keep going.

Perform throughout the process.

In the initial round of playoffs, that season,

Heat was then forced to face the New York Knicks. Heat

They won in five games. It was so impressive!

They were able to win every game by over 10 points.

points. They focus and are intense at another level. In

The second round of playoffs was their final.

Indiana Pacers. LeBron put in his best against the Pacers.

He had 32 points, 15 rebounds, 5 assists and 5 steals. He was the team's leader

to a 95-86 win. Indiana won the next two matches.

They are intense and can beat the Heat. LeBron is serious

necessary to evaluate the team's strategy or they could

End up with an early exit In Game 4, the team came

The Heat beat the Pacers 101 - 93 together. The Heat continued

They were able to win the Game 5 & 6 in complete blowouts. They

They defeated the Pacers 115 to83 in Game 5 as well as 105 to93 in Game 9.

Game 6. They were hungry to win that championship. They were eager for the championship.

Game 4: Everyone knew why LeBron is the King, as he was.

He finished with 40 points and 18 rebounds. Just one

Avert a nasty triple double in a playoff.

The Heat would continue to face the Celtics during the

Eastern Conference Finals. It would be one.

Amazing playoff matchups. A performance by the

decades. Game 1 against Celtics ended up being a

It was a complete blowout when the Heat beat the Heat 93 to 79. The Heat

She dominated all ends of this floor. LeBron dropped 32

The team had 13 rebounds and 3 assists, for a total of 11 points. Dwyane was awarded a

Solid performance with 22 points and 7 assists.

Game 2 ended up being close, but the Heat won.

out and won. Final score was 115-111.

They were becoming closer to the finish line.

Finals again. Game 3 would be a difficult one.

The Celtics beat the Heat 101-91.

Game 4 was close, and both the players and the referee were able to win.

Each team displayed exceptional defense and offense. LeBron

This game ended with 29 points, 6 rebound and 3 assists.

assists. Dwyane also played a solid 20-minute game.

Six assists, 7 rebounds and seven points. It was an excellent game, even though it was not a

In a close game, Heat lost 93 to 91. The series concluded.

Now they were tied 2-2, and the pressure was rising for

The Heat. The Celtics didn't give up.

Strategies to beat them with heat are essential. Game

5 was another close one. LeBron played to his heart's content

He was able to score 30 points, 13 rebound and 2 assists. His

It was not enough. They continued to lose.

Game 5 finished with a final score between 94 and 90. The Heat were now

Only one game to go before they lose the entire series. If they

To win that championship they needed to look to their own records.

leader. LeBron needed to perform in Game 6 or else they would

be returned to you packed. LeBron had one game in Game 6.

He has the best playoff performances in his career, bringing in 45

Points, 15 rebounds and five assists. He simply refused to

Heat defeated the Heat 98-79. It was now

Game 7 is now and the stakes are higher.

This is more than ever. Is LeBron able to lead his team?

To advance to the Finals, they must win over the Celtics.

Everyone started to analyze and predict.

LeBron would fall to the floor under the weight. LeBron didn't

was not concerned about critics who doubted his character and was solely

He was determined to help his team win. Game 7

LeBron was relentless when it came to getting to the rim. He scored 31

Scored points, 12 rebounds, 2 assists. Dwyane D Wade had 23

6 rebounds and 6 assist. The game started at

Although it was slow, things started to pick up during the 2nd quarter. It was

From the beginning of the second half, it was a tight game.

The heat started to slowly recede and shut down.

Celtics defensively. Chris Bosh was clutch during the 3

Point line in the 3rd quarter and 4th quarters and the Heat

They were able to overcome the odds and take the victory.

The final score of game was 101-88. The Heat were

We are heading to the NBA finals once again.

LeBron was focused, determined, and determined to keep the team together.

He was not the champion this year. The Heat were

They play like a championship side team and were once

They were once again at the finals, where they wanted. They were

Faced with the Oklahoma City Thunder in finals

Kevin Durant, a rising star, could do anything. He

He could shoot anywhere he wanted

You can drive the lane, score effortlessly, and be a driver.

A defensive threat. He would be a tough opponent.

LeBron was the matchup and there were no doubts that the

Finals were going be filled with outstanding performances

competition. Russell Westbrook was also part of the Thunder.

Their point guard was aggressive, explosive, and a great teammate.

We would do anything just to win. Durant, Westbrook were

Both All-Stars who wanted to win were just as desperate as

LeBron. The real question was: Who was going to win?

Be the 2012 NBA Champion Team?

As the finals approached, it was still unclear who would win.

They really did win. In the regular series, the series were tied.

At 1-1. Both teams were equally stacked against one another

Other than what most experts and analysts could see,

But you can still argue. Just wait to see how it all unfolds in the finals.

Game 1 began in the fast-paced style that reflects this style of play.

Thunder were used a lot to playing. They were running

Spread the floor and move aggressively towards the basket.

Kevin Durant performed brilliantly with 36 points, 8

4 assists, and 3 rebounds. He proved to have serious problems

LeBron would be in fierce competition. Westbrook could also go on to

You had a good night with 27 points (8 rebounds) and 11 points (11).

assists. LeBron concluded Game 1 scoring 30 points.

4 assists and rebounds. The Thunder proved to be the

The better team won Game 1 by 105 to 94. It

That was the kind of game that had cost them their lives

The past is the past. LeBron was determined that he would not

Let it happen again. Game 2 would be even more exciting.

Tough game, but Heat won.

100-96. It was a tight game and everyone won.

Both teams seemed hungry to see the results.

championship. LeBron finished Game 2 on 32 points, 8

5 assists and rebounds. Dwyane Wade contributed 24

Heats win points. Game 3 was another.

Battle for the two teams. The Heat came out on top

The Heat won again the game, 91-85. The Heat were playing

smart basketball, and they knew it if they tried to play.

At the speed that Durant and Westbrook were going, they would

be at a disadvantage. They realized this in Game 1

You decided to slow down play and throw the ball.

Thunder on their game. In Game 4, the Heat knew that they

They did their best to keep their heads up.

You can control the flow of your game. They knew that if they did, they could manage the flow of play.

They were going be victorious. It was slow to start, but it quickly became a fast-paced game.

The second half began to pick-up.

Westbrook driving aggressively to the basket

Westbrook was the winner with 43 points.

Heat managed to take control of the game in their favor.

Ended up winning 104-98. LeBron didn't cave in.

The leader in the beginning of things was him.

tough. Between the

LeBron realized that his team required a 4th and 3rd quarters.

He needed to be a leader, and he was willing to step up. He completed the night.

With 26 points and 9 rebounds. One rebound

A triple-double is unattainable. The Heat were now one

LeBron is just one game away from becoming NBA champions

His first ring was only one game away. He has not yet received his first ring.

No team in NBA history has ever been able to recover from a 3-1 loss.

The Heat were unable to overcome a deficit in the finals and win it. The Heat were no strangers

to luck and Cinderella stories. They knew they weren't.

going to let this happen. Thunder needed a miracle

To win. In Game 5, the Thunder looked tired and defeated.

And they were not ready for play. The Heat took full advantage.

The winner was 121-106. LeBron was a true professional and completed his task.

Triple double, a game consisting 26 points, 11

13 assists, and 11 rebounds. The Heat won the 2012 NBA

champs and LeBron had finally won the first of his kind

championship. LeBron's journey.

His first NBA championship win was finally achieved.

Although he faced many difficulties, he eventually became a champion. After

LeBron was the next one up when the game was finished.

Bill Russell is one the greatest basketball players of all times.

He was awarded 2012 NBA finals MVP. All

His hard work, sacrifices and public scrutiny.

The hard work was well worth it. LeBron James was finally a NBA member

champion.

2012-2013 Season

Following their title win, the Miami Heat

The team that everyone wanted was the one to beat. They now

You had a winning mindset and foundation for the next step.

Season and even more. People were comparing

LeBron has been the great Michael Jordan eversince he arrived

In the league. After winning his first title, it was

Being a reality was possible because he had all the skills and determination

passion to be better than MJ. How would his

How is success in the NBA measured? Is it by the

He won how many championships, how many points

The score he got, or the impact it would have had on the team

What is the game of basketball? It was not clear at this point.

LeBron was undoubtedly one of the most outstanding.

He would continue to play for the league with his players

Be determined to achieve greatness

The Heat had some success in the 2012-2013 Season

They made changes to their roster to add strength

They are versatile. They realized that they lacked outside.

It could have cost them their playoffs game

championship. They needed a veteran who was a

A 3-point shooter with a clutch shot and who wouldn't hesitate to take a chance on a

Shot when the game is on. You can't go wrong with bringing on

Ray Allen, one of the greatest 3-point shooters of all-time, is Ray Allen.

Ray Allen had won a Boston championship

Celtics had an obsessive work ethic similar to that of the Heat.

Chapter 18: I'm Coming Home

LeBron was released following the Heat's loss.

The agent could be freed and there was plenty of speculation.

It was what he planned to do. Many believed that he would.

Because of his success with the Heat, he would be resigning.

He shared his love for them and the close relationship he had with Chris Bosh

Dwayne. He could choose to stay in Miami and pursue his dream.

You could see him return to the Big 3 for more championships.

Cleveland, bring it home!

championship. Media speculations

All analysts were positive that LeBron would go home.

They were correct in Cleveland.

Season 2014-2015

LeBron made his final decision and returned home.

Cleveland. Cleveland.

Their king to return home to his family. LeBron

He returned to Cleveland as an older leader.

player. He knew that only raw talent was not enough.

enough to help bring a title to the city

Cleveland. He knew that he needed a team in order to share the task.

Take his vision and be open to doing the hard work

It would turn a team from a mere group of people into champions. You know what it takes to be a champion?

You must be willing to sacrifice for your work and you must be open to learning.

All aspects of the game.

LeBron announced his resignation in the weeks that followed.

His return to Cleveland is accompanied by talks about acquiring the city.

Kevin Love emerged. Their plan was for a

Triple threat in Cleveland including LeBron and Kevin

Love and one among the top point guards of the league.

Kyrie Irving. After much speculation, it was finally done by the Cavs

Kevin Love officially announced that he would be joining them in the

2014 season. The Cleveland Cavaliers looked fantastic

LeBron and Kevin Love were among the guests. Kyrie Irving was also there

They were the leaders of their team. James now had to get to work.

It's hard to bring home a trophy to the city.

Cleveland. LeBron Jam a.k.a "The Chosen One", better known as

The "Kids from Akron", the "Kid from Akron", was back home in his hometown

Willing to do whatever it takes for his city.

LeBron's debut game back in Cleveland

The result would be unmistakable. More than 20,000 loyal

LeBron was greeted warmly by the fans as he returned to the venue through the front door.

Tunnels to the Quicken Loans Arena. LeBron and Cavs

The group received a standing ovation as they entered the building.

LeBron's greatest moment was in this role.

Cleveland fans and Cleveland were ready for them

To return home, the king. The entire first quarter

LeBron was cheered by his fans every moment.

He got the ball every single time. The Cavs faced

New York Knicks in their season opener.

Losing 95-90, the energy which came from fans

They set the tone and direction for the rest of the season. Even

The Cavs did not lose their season opener but the king was

He's back, ready to fulfill his promise for the city of

Cleveland and bring back that championship

The Cavs experienced a slow start.

regular season lost 3 of the first 5 games.

Four consecutive losses between their 9th- and 12th games

game. This caused a lot more criticism from sports.

Analysts, commentators, and others. They began to state that the

Cavs didn't have it in their system, and LeBron was.

Not the leader he was when he was in Miami. The Cavs would

Finally things will turn around and 8 consecutive wins are achieved

After their losses, they started to play in games. They began to play in greater numbers.

Everything started to look positive when everyone worked together.

them. LeBron's regular season is thirty-two games in.

began to experience muscle strains at his lower extremities

back and pain in the knees. It was that which caused him 8 missed.

You can play games between December 30th 2014 and January 11, 2014.

2015 LeBron was absent for 8 games. The Cavs replaced him with the Cavs

He played badly and lost seven games. His absence

He was able to show how crucial the Cavs needed his win. After he

When he returned from injury, the Cavs won 11

two games in one. It was obvious LeBron's presence.

For the Cavs' to succeed, the court had to be used.

Perform at your peak.

LeBron came back from Mexico around the exact same time.

The Cavs acquired shooting after his injury.

Iman Shumpert will be guarded by the Knicks Iman Schumpert

Cavs needed him as a defensive player.

They needed someone who could help defend their players.

Shumpert would continue to fill that area of the perimeter.

void. They also bought J.R. Smith.

Knicks is an athletic small-guard who could shoot from any position.

Three. Drive aggressively to the lane while defending like no one else.

other. They had a better lineup and were hungry.

they would ever be able to pursue the title. They would finish.

The regular season was a 53-29 record. They were finished

First in NBA Central Division.

Eastern Conference People began to wonder:

What would happen if LeBron were to become ill?

The same injuries were sustained in the playoffs. Even though it wasn't,

LeBron wanted a record like the Cavs.

The team was confident and ready to play in the playoffs.

The Cavs then faced the Boston Celtics.

They won the first round and were swept by them in four playoffs.

games. The Cavs played like an All Star team.

The Celtics were easily beaten by them. Their

Second round of playoffs against an improved

Chicago Bulls team, who gave them a tough time. The

Cavs would nevertheless win and beat them in

Six games. Their next series is against the Atlanta Hawks

was supposed to be hard, but the Cavs won.

They won four of their remaining games. They were victorious in four of their final games.

They defeated them in game 4 by 30 point and the way they

Play made everyone think that this was the best year ever.

They would win a title.

The Cavs faced off with the Golden State in the finals

Warriors who enjoyed one of their best seasons

franchise history. They relied on their quick ball.

Movement and consistent three-point shooting are key to winning games. It made it extremely difficult for other team to

correctly adjust on defense. Their style of play is

Teams were extremely efficient and speedy and fell apart.

They won against them. They were often able blow teams apart by 20-30

point. The finals would, one thing was certain.

The battle between them, and the Cavaliers, would be fierce.

LeBron had an assist in Game 1 against Warriors

unforgettable night. He dropped 44 points, 8 rebound

And 6 assists. The Warriors defense was unable to stop him.

He attempted 18 field goals and 2 more.

8 three-pointers. Kyrie Irving closed the night scoring 23.

The game ended with 6 assists, 7 rebounds and points. The final 2:20 is left to enter the game the Cavaliers did not expect what

It was the next. Kyrie Irving went down, and started.

He fell to the ground. He left the game.

And headed straight to the locker area. Despite

LeBron's excellent performance was not enough to win the Cavs

And they lost Game 1 by eight points. Following Game 1 news

Kyrie Irving will be attending the festivities, according to reports

Fractured kneecaps prevented me from competing in the finals After

Kyrie made the following announcements

message to his Instagram fans "I just want to say thank you."

Many thanks to all for the well wishes. I was saddened by your actions.

You had to go out, but that doesn't make it any less enjoyable.

part of a special playoff race with my brothers. Truly

Thanks for your support and love. It was all my fault.

Everything I did and still do. This game is one of my favorites.

I won't let you down and I'll see you soon. To my brothers

"You already know what the deal means." The Cavs star point

Guard could not help them fight for their title

LeBron felt the pressure again this year.

Kyrie was there for the remainder of the evening

Finals, LeBron determined to run for the championship

title. In Game 2, he made an amazing triple double

Comprising 39 points, 16 rebounds, 11 assists The

Steph might have made Cavs luck in Game 2 because they may have won the game.

Curry's terrible shooting night. Curry managed to make 5

The field goal percentage was 23 and the three-pointer percentage was 2 of 15. The

Cavs won overtime against Warriors 95-93 In

Game 3 Steph curry had an incredible shooting night

Sunk 7 of 13 3-pointers and made 10 out of 20

field goals. LeBron had an amazing career.

night dropped 40 points and had 12 rebounds as well as 8 assists. He

It was only 2 assists short of a back-to back triple double.

The Cavs won Game 3 with a final score

96-91. They did not have their leading point guard.

They were playing well together, and the ball was distributed well. The

Cavs had some achievements

momentum from the last two games, and we hoped that it will carry us in

Game 4. Game 4.

It was very different from the tip off. The Warriors offense

Games 2/3 became boring, but they shifted the blame.

For more pick and rolls, their offense should be paced faster

They're not the same as they used to be. This

The Cavaliers were taken by surprise, and they didn't know it.

Correctly adjust their play to win. They

LeBron was only allowed to score 20 points. This made it embarrassing for him.

Cavaliers with a win of 103 to 82 It was clear that it was the Cavaliers who won 103-82.

Cavaliers defense had been a weak point for Warriors.

It and took full advantage. The Cavs

LeBron must change their style of play, or they will be punished.

be in serious danger. LeBron was able to continue his stellar career.

triple double performance in Game 5, dropping 40

His performance included 11 assists, 14 rebounds and points. His performance

However, the Cavaliers would not win.

Steph Curry was in absolute blaze mode on the field

Game 5, 37 points down He finished 7 of 13

He attempted three-pointers. LeBron did not have a

Warriors gave a fantastic performance in Game 5

They won by 13 points. Game 5's final score was

104-91. The Cavs were now one game away

They won't let the championship pass them. They

They needed to change their style of playing if they were to succeed.

of winning the championship. LeBron had 32 during Game 6.

He finished with 9 assists, 18 rebound and 10 points. He had an absolutely

Although the Cavaliers gave a stellar performance, they fell short

The Warriors won the game 105-97. The Warriors became the

2015 NBA Champions Despite Cavs' loss to Warriors

LeBron was outstanding in the finals.

Record books. He averaged 35.8 points and 13.3 boards.

8.8 assists. LeBron realized why Cavs lost to them

Warriors and was determined that it would not happen

again. He realized that they didn't properly adjust their

You can play as a whole team. It was evident to analysts and fans.

LeBron and Kyrie were crucial to the Cavs.

In order to win a title, they must work together. Would

What will they do next year to make it possible?

Season 2015-2016

The Cavaliers wanted to maintain their existing plans.

Their previous season's winning lineup.

Even though the Cavs made the Finals the previous year,

They began to crumble once the Warriors adjusted them

style of play. LeBron intended to improve his play this season.

Team spirit between all to achieve

You are able to adapt to any situation. LeBron recognised this.

The Cavs had a lack of consistency when they played.

He gained momentum. He intended to work with the

To finally win a championship, we needed a team.

Cleveland.

There were no other teams in this league like it.

Cavaliers as well as the Warriors. They were the top two.

Champion-hungry people and teams are strongly encouraged

They believed that they would fight again

Finals.

The Cavs kicked off their season by winning

15 of their first twenty games. Their improvement over

Anyone who had seen the previous season could see it.

They play. The whole team was getting together and playing

Better than ever, even though Kyrie Irving hasn't been running

That's the point. Kyrie returned for the 25th season game

Following his final injury, he got off to a strong start. His

Cleveland faced the opposition in his first game back after his injury

Philadelphia 76'ers. It was obvious how much more the

Cavs played Irving with great success.

76'ers, 22 points. Shortly after Kyrie Irving's

In return, the Cavs won an impressive eight-game series

streak. It looked good until midway.

Through the season, when they lost more

games. Consistency was a problem that they encountered in the finals

They were being spied on again. Despite LeBron

His best game of basketball was the

The team started to struggle. The Cavs felt they had to have a

A positive change would help them.

They had to be ready for the playoffs. They didn't have to

A lineup adjustment is not enough. Management is also required.

adjustment.

Timofey mozgov was their start center.

Not as well as they expected.

planned. He was not the kind of offensive and defensive guy you might expect.

They needed to be able to rely on the starting center for their threat. They needed

Someone to make an announcement in the post.

If it was really important, aggressive. David Blatt

Tristan Thompson, 6'9 inches tall, was overtaken by Tristan Thompson.

Timofey Mozgov. Tristan Thompson proved that he

Could score well in paint and be an aggressive player

defensive force. Before he was promoted to his first position

He was averaging about 8 points and 10 rebounds each.

game. He was a reliable off-the-benches player and with

His position in the starting five would not be occupied by the Cavs.

There is improvement towards the end.

David Blatt was the no. 1 management coach.

While he isn't a stranger when it comes to winning, he wasn't the kind of coach who would.

They were urgently needed by the Cavaliers. He was a major force

They were instrumental in getting the Cavs to finals. The issue was

LeBron, he and he never really reached an agreement on how the deal should be done.

Cavs needed to play in championship.

Coach Blatt helped save a struggling Cleveland

LeBron wasn't part of the team, so they had to form a team.

LeBron suddenly leaps to the NBA finals in his first season

He wasn't prepared to come home.

for. They showed mutual respect for each other.

They knew inside that it was time for a

change.

Tristan Thompson moved to the next day.

Assistant coach Tyron Lue was placed in the middle position.

David Blatt was appointed head coach of Cavs.

let go. Tyron Lune was a younger coach with a positive attitude

That was what the other players loved. The other players enjoyed it.

Improvements in their starting line-up and a new Head

Cavs coach, they felt they had made all the necessary adjustments.

We will make adjustments to make the season complete strong.

Get ready to play in the playoffs. They finished 1st at the NBA

Eastern Conference with a record 57-25 for the season.

LeBron averaged 25.3 Points and 7.4 Rebounds in the season.

6.8 assists per play

They faced the opposition in the first round of playoffs.

Detroit Pistons that they were able beat in a 4

game sweep. LeBron played well in all those

You can play games, take smart shots, and average over 50%

The field. Kyrie Irving played exceptionally well in the field.

The first round playoffs. In the first four rounds, against

On an average game with the Pistons, he scored 27.5 points

Incredible 47% shooting from a field. Kevin Love was

Additionally, the average double-double is also extremely impressive.

Through the first 4 games and scoring more than 18 per game

game.

In the second round of playoffs, they were faced with

Atlanta Hawks LeBron and Cavs were fine

They beat the Hawks by four games. They beat them in four games.

Hawks beat by 11 points, 25 points and 13 points in Game 1.

Points in Game 3 and 1 in Game 4 They were

We were absolutely unstoppable. We were determined to win

This season, the title.

In the Eastern Conference finals, Cavs faced

Toronto Raptors The Cavs lost Game 1 to the Toronto Raptors.

They beat the Raptors 31-points.

They had now won 9 consecutive playoffs games, and were

They were hungry for the 10th. This was how they were able to play

In order to win championship. In Game 1 LeBron

He scored 24 points in only 28 minutes. His

Efficiency in the playoffs was something that you'd only dream of.

game. Kyrie Irving added 27 more points to the Cavs win

Kevin Love added 14 points. The Cavs went on

Their 10th win was easy, as they won Game 2 without any difficulty

consecutive playoff win. It was a remarkable performance.

Record books The Cavs lost in Games 3 & 4.

The defensive side lost both of the games. The series were

The Raptors tied the game at 2-2.

An unbroken streak of victories in the playoffs. The Cavs quickly realized the importance of this.

They couldn't let go of their beloved.

They had momentum before. In Game 5, they will be able to maintain their momentum.

www.ingramcontent.com/pod-product-compliance
Lightning Source LLC
Chambersburg PA
CBHW050405120526
44590CB00015B/1835